Training to Win
Football

Training to Win
Football

Rolf Wirhed

Department of Physical Education
University of Örebro
Sweden

Wolfe Publishing

Copyright © Wolfe Publishing, 1992
Published by Wolfe Publishing, an imprint of Mosby–Year Book Europe Ltd, 1992
Printed by BPCC Hazells Ltd, Aylesbury, England
ISBN 0 7234 1778 4

A CIP catalogue record for this book is available from the British Library.

For full details of all Mosby–Year Book Europe Ltd titles, please write to Mosby–Year Book Europe Ltd, Brook House, 2–16 Torrington Place, London WC1E 7LT, England.

Contents

Introduction

To become a good footballer you need, among other things, strength, flexibility, speed, skill with the ball, and tactical vision. Football demands a great deal of the skilful professional, but it can also be played by most people at an amateur level. Amateur players have contributed a lot to making football the world's most popular sport.

In this book you will learn which muscles are the most important when it comes to running, jumping, kicking and heading. Then you will learn the various ways of training these muscles. This should help you become a better player and give you much more chance of avoiding unnecessary injuries.

THE STRUCTURE OF THE MUSCLES AND HOW THEY WORK

To understand how to train, first you need to know a little about how muscles work. A muscle consists of muscle cells, tendons and connective tissue. Muscle cells are able to contract and shorten in length by about 50%, i.e. the muscle becomes short and thick (**Figure 1**). Muscle extension is prevented by the connective tissue (**Figure 2**).

The strength of a muscle depends on the number of cells it contains and their thickness. When you exercise, you teach the body to:

- Use these cells.
- Supply the cells with oxygen so that they can carry out the same movement time after time for a long period.
- Force the muscle to build up each cell so that it becomes a little thicker; in other words, a little stronger.

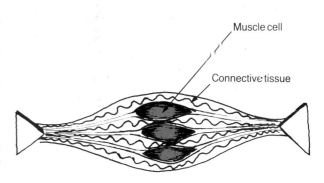

Figure 1 When the muscle cells contract the connective tissue is loose and creased.

Figure 2 The muscle extended with the connective tissue rigid and tense.

To achieve the first two effects, easy exercises performed many times are enough. To achieve thicker and therefore stronger muscles, you have to put everything you can into the exercise so that the muscle is forced to carry out movements which it can only just manage. The muscle must be forced to work at 100% capacity. This will be explained in more detail on page 57.

As the muscle gets stronger it builds up stronger connective tissue, so that it can withstand the stresses that the muscle cells may now expose it to. The muscle might otherwise 'pull itself apart'. This sometimes happens and you suffer a ruptured muscle. Although muscle cells grow quite quickly with hard training, connective tissue takes longer. You have to build up your strength, therefore, by certain well-tried methods so that progress is not too quick. A suitable training schedule is set out on page 85.

Muscles that are so placed that they affect the same joint but produce opposite movements are called each other's antagonists. A muscle that extends the knee is the antagonist of one that flexes the knee. **Figure 3** shows how a muscle called the biceps femoris pulls the lower leg backwards when it contracts (flexes the knee) at the same time as a muscle on the front of the thigh (rectus femoris) follows with the movement. This happens when, for instance, you lift your lower leg in preparation for a hard kick. When you make contact the situation is precisely the reverse. The rectus femoris contracts sharply, so that the lower leg is pushed forward at the same time as the muscle on the back of the thigh follows through passively without obstructing the movement. If you want to shoot hard the front muscle must be strong; at the same time, the back muscle must not be too rigid and short.

There is evidence that a muscle which has been drawn out to 20% more than its resting length will develop its greatest possible force when it is about to contract again. A great many football players have insufficient flexibility to utilise this effect fully. Evidence also suggests that a muscle should be drawn relatively quickly to this 20% longer stage to reach the greatest force possible. By means of stretching you can make it possible for the muscle to be drawn out long enough, while jerks and elastic stretching make it possible to do so with speed and muscle strength. Consequently, the stretching exercises on pages 43–47 should be combined with elastic stretching and jerks.

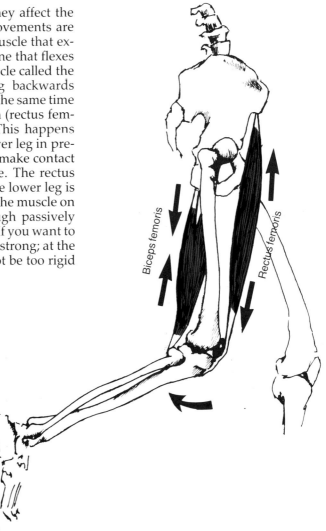

Figure 3 This is how the muscles work when bending your knee.

2 Anatomy

'FOOTBALL MUSCLES'

Now you are going to learn what muscles are important to a football player: their names, where they are situated and when and how they work when you are playing. The intention is that you should understand why you should train these muscles and how to do so.

We will look at the following muscles:

- The hip extensors.
- The knee extensors.
- The thigh muscles.
- The calf muscle.
- The knee flexors.

- The hip flexors.
- The groin muscles.
- The back muscles.
- The stomach muscles.

The hip extensors

The main hip extensor (gluteus maximus) is called the large buttock muscle and is one of the strongest muscles of the body (**Figure 4**). You use this muscle when you simultaneously straighten your hip and knee. Consequently, it is activated by quick starting and jumping and when you are running and want to accelerate. Think about how you act when you want to increase speed. You bend somewhat more forward at the hip (i.e. the large buttock muscle is drawn out a little, up to the 20% extension mentioned on page 55) to make it possible for the muscle to work with greater force in the backward drive of the leg.

The gluteus maximus is in a class of its own as the strongest hip extensor muscle but it is helped by several other muscles, including the the gluteus medius (**Figure 5**) and the gluteus minimus (**Figure 6**). These muscles sit at an angle in front of

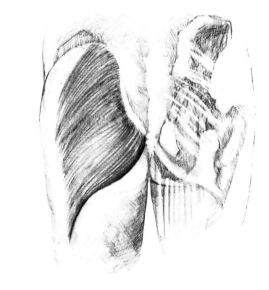

Figure 4 Large buttock muscle (gluteus maximus).

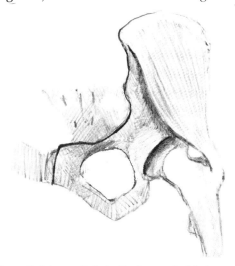

Figure 5 Intermediate buttock muscle (gluteus medius).

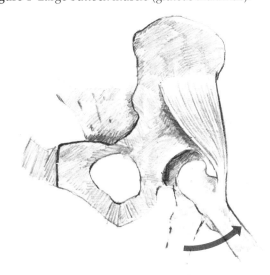

Figure 6 Small buttock muscle (gluteus minimus).

Figure 7

Figure 8

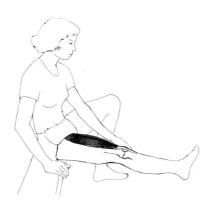

Figure 9

the gluteus maximus and, because they have such a wide range, they can swing the leg back (stretch the hip) or forward (bend the hip). Nerve cells in the brain stimulate the muscle cells in the front parts of the muscle to swing the leg forwards, while corresponding action on muscle cells in the back part of the muscle swings the leg back. The gluteus medius provides the the strength for landing on one leg and for making quick changes of direction while running. Under the gluteus medius is the gluteus minimus, which acts in the same way. These two muscles, which help each other to carry out movements, are called agonists (the opposite of antagonists).

The knee extensors

The knee extensor, shown with the muscle maximally shortened in **Figure 7**, is called the straight thigh muscle. It straightens the knee and flexes the hip, i.e. exactly what happens when you are about to kick the ball hard.

Standing like the girl in **Figure 8**, with an angle of 90° at the hip and the leg straight, you will soon find out how it feels to get lactic acid in the straight thigh muscle. It is good if you are able to lift your leg up to an angle of 90°. If you cannot do this it is because the muscles at the back of your thigh and knee are too short. You will probably feel how the muscle struggles against the movement there. If you stand trying to lift your leg like this for 5–10 seconds you will soon feel a pain at the front of your thigh. This is because the muscle which lifts the leg and straightens the knee has to work statically so hard that no blood can reach the muscle. The blood vessels are squeezed together and blocked by the contracted and thick muscle. The energy that the muscle needs is now produced without the oxygen of the blood, in a process that produces lactic acid as a waste product. If the production of lactic acid becomes too high there will be a pain in the muscle and you will need to relax in order to let the blood pass. This will allow oxygen to reach the muscle.

Try sitting with one leg straight out and the heel resting against the floor, as shown in **Figure 9**. See how much you can move the kneecap in various directions. The kneecap is a part of the muscle and functions as a strengthener. Without the kneecap the muscle would be worn too severely on the thigh bone in deep knee flexions. If it is possible to move the kneecap to and fro with the muscle relaxed, try to lift your heel from the floor and still have a 'loose' kneecap. You will probably find that this is impossible. The rectus femoris, which helps to lift the leg, must be tensed and then the kneecap is automatically pulled upwards. The kneecap is embedded in the muscle tendon and follows along with the movement. The thickness and position of the kneecap mean that the tendon is lifted outwards and forwards in relation to the centre of the knee joint (**Figure 10**). In this way the muscle gets a better leverage on the joint and can thus cope with greater loads. You simply get stronger.

The thigh muscles

Apart from the rectus femoris (**Figure 11**), three other muscles also come to the kneecap. These are called the vastus lateralis (**Figure 12**), the vastus intermedius (**Figure 13**) and the vastus medialis (**Figure 14**). The outer muscle can be felt on the outside of the thigh, the middle muscle is hidden behind the straight thigh muscle, while the inner muscle is seen as a 'pouch' on the inside of the thigh just above the kneecap. These three muscles stretch the knee but cannot affect movement in the hip in the same way as the rectus femoris. Together with the rectus femoris the three muscles comprise the quadriceps femoris muscle of the thigh.

The calf muscle

The calf muscle in **Figure 15** comprises the gastrocnemius, which starts from the thigh bone, and the soleus, which is inside and further down; the soleus does not pass the knee joint, only the ankle joint. Together, the gastrocnemius and soleus enable you to rise up on your toes, run without putting your heels to the ground, kick forwards while running along and jump up in the air. A powerful player usually has strong calf muscles.

The muscle and, therefore, its tendon, which is called the Achilles tendon (after the great warrior of Greek mythology), is exposed to great stresses. The tendon does rupture sometimes, but this is usually preceded by pain or tenderness. So be careful, and do not train if you get a pain in your 'heel' when you put any strain on it.

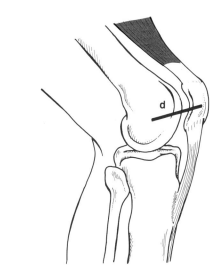

Figure 10

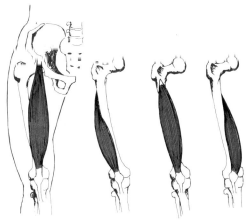

Figures 11–14   The thigh muscles.

Figure 15

Figure 16

The knee flexors

This group of muscles works quickly and with considerable force when you run. Immediately the foot leaves the ground in a running step, the lower leg is pulled up so that your heel almost hits your buttocks. The faster this happens the faster the leg is bent double and the faster it swings forward. Torn muscles in the back of the thigh are very common and are best prevented with gentle training combined with active stretching. The stretching exercises are described on page 47.

The knee flexors in **Figure 16** are also called hamstrings and comprise three different muscles. At the back of the knee you can feel one tendon on the outside and two on the inside. All three muscles start from the ischial tuberosity, which is behind the hip joint. When the muscle contracts the knee bends and you stretch your hip. The same thing happens when you are preparing to take a kick (see **Figure 30**).

The hip flexors

The main hip flexing muscle in **Figure 17** is called the iliopsoas and is responsible for swinging the thigh forwards quickly, as when running. This muscle is sometimes called the sprinter muscle. The muscle must be supple so that it does not prevent the thigh from actually stretching out backwards in kicking away when you are running full-speed ahead. A stiff foreshortened muscle produces a short 'pace' and places a strain on the lower part of the vertebral column with each running step. Pains and stiffness in the lumbar region and an inability to run fast may well be due to untrained and foreshortened hip flexors.

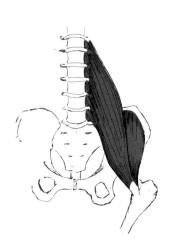

Figure 17

The groin muscles

The muscle shown in **Figure 18** is one of five muscles which together form the muscles of the groin. If these muscles are too weak, injuries may easily occur when running quickly or kicking with the inside of the foot, a so-called broadside. These muscles are exposed to very severe strains in a tackle. The groin muscles should be exposed to regular stretching and gentle bodybuilding training in order to prevent damage. Groin injuries are very difficult to overcome and are often expressed in inflammation, with pain in the area of the root of the muscle, i.e. the pubic bone (os pubis). If the groin muscles are too short you cannot reach the correct pace when you want to run fast.

Figure 18

The back muscles

The small and large muscles that straighten the back, twist the thorax and bend the thorax to the side are collectively known as the back muscles or erector spinae (**Figure 19**). They are very important for stabilizing the delicate vertebral column. Some of these muscles are shown in **Figures 20–22**.

Figure 19

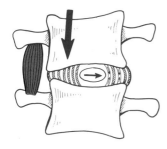

Figure 20 This back muscle helps in bending sideways.

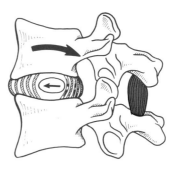

Figure 21 This muscle straightens the spine.

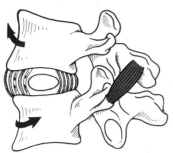

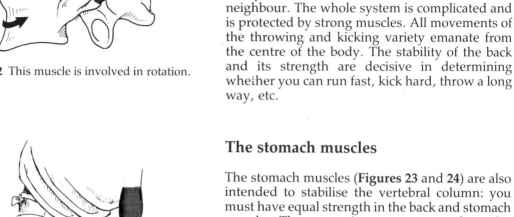

Figure 22 This muscle is involved in rotation.

The back muscles mainly connect the vertebrae. The shortest muscles go from one vertebra to the next. Others pass several vertebrae before they are attached, the longest passing up to nine vertebrae. Between the vertebrae are shock-absorbing flexible discs, which allow each vertebra to tilt a little in any direction and to turn a little in relation to its neighbour. The whole system is complicated and is protected by strong muscles. All movements of the throwing and kicking variety emanate from the centre of the body. The stability of the back and its strength are decisive in determining whether you can run fast, kick hard, throw a long way, etc.

The stomach muscles

The stomach muscles (**Figures 23** and **24**) are also intended to stabilise the vertebral column: you must have equal strength in the back and stomach muscles. They are an important group of muscles which protect the spine and stabilise movements. **Figure 23** shows the rectus abdominis, which when contracted makes you bend forward (or prevents the spine from being pulled forward). **Figure 24** shows the external oblique abdominal muscle, which starts at the right side of the chest and extends to the left side of the pelvic girdle, where it is fixed by a tendon. Under this muscle you can see the internal oblique abdominal muscle, which starts at the left side of the pelvic girdle and extends to the right side of the chest where it is fixed by a tendon. Both of these muscles are working at the same time when you lie on your back and do a twisted sit-up so that your right shoulder moves towards your left leg. The same muscles work when you kick a shot with your left foot or when you swing your left leg forward in running. Then you have to twist the right part of the thorax forward. This is taken care of by the muscles shown in **Figure 24**; the harder you kick and the quicker you want to run, the stronger these muscles should be. Precisely the same set of muscles is to be found on the right side of the body of course but these are not shown in **Figure 24**.

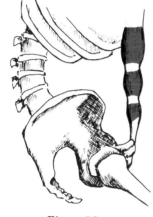

Figure 23

Figure 24

3 Analysis of Running, Kicking, Heading and Power

RUNNING

Important muscles when running

Figures 25 and **26–28** show the positions of the supporting leg and the swinging leg when running. At the start you straighten the supporting leg with great force, at both the hip joint and the knee joint as well as at the ankle joint. The muscles of the supporting leg which have to be strong are shown in **Figure 25**:

(a) The large buttock muscle, which straightens the hip.
(b) The knee extensors which straighten the knee.
(c) The calf muscle, which straightens the ankle.

The swinging leg is vigorously pulled forward, engaging other muscles:

(d) The knee flexors.
(e) The hip flexors.

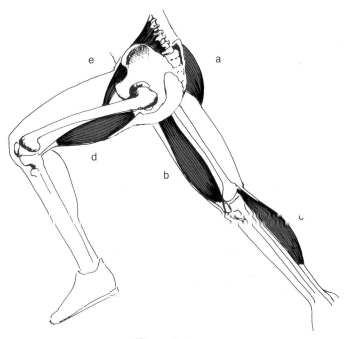

Figure 25

The swing phase of the leg during running

When running a long distance you swing the leg with a rather small flexion of the knee. During fast running, however, you have to be able to flex the leg much more and thereby lift the lower leg behind you as much as possible. This will make it easier for the hip flexors (the long lumbar muscle) to swing the leg forward again quickly. When running with a ball you take shorter steps than usual, so that you can control and kick the ball. You widen the distance between your feet in order to dribble or to come to the correct position for passing or shooting. This way of running is not good for moving a long distance on the football ground quickly. Accordingly, you can distinguish between three types of running:

● Slow running without a ball (**Figure 26**). There is a relatively small knee flexion in the forward swing of the leg and your foot strikes the ground on the outer border of your heel. A backward drive occurs, from the big toe border of your foot.
● Fast running without a ball (**Figure 27**). There is a greater flexion of the knee in the forward

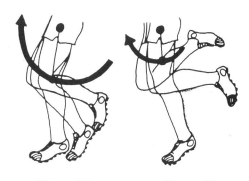

Figure 26   **Figure 27**

swing. Your heel is almost against your buttocks and your foot strikes the ground with the front of the foot. A backward drive of the leg occurs, with a proper hip extension.

- Running with a ball (**Figure 28**). Short steps are taken, with a fairly wide gap between the feet. Your foot strikes the ground with the whole foot. You control the ball and are prepared for stopping, changing direction and acceleration. The position is somewhat flexed at the hip and also in the backward drive of the leg.

Hamstrings

Figure 29 shows the muscles that can quickly swing up the lower part of the leg. They originate from the lowermost part of the hip bone, the ischial tuberosity. The muscles and their tendons can easily be felt at the back of the thigh and the knee joint. They are inserted at the back of the lower leg. The collective name for these muscles, three in all, is the hamstrings. **Figure 30** shows a position of the leg where the hamstrings are maximally contracted and **Figure 31** a position where they are maximally stretched. In **Figure 30** the hamstrings are used for drawing out and charging the knee extensor for a shot, while in **Figure 31** they are engaged in halting the lower part of the leg before the muscle is drawn out so far that it snaps.

In general, football players can be said to have short hamstrings. It is known that a muscle gradually shortens when used very often under heavy stress. This is because the connective tissue becomes thicker and shorter if you only train muscle strength without stretching your muscles afterwards. It is especially important to maintain the length of these muscles if you want to avoid injuries and to run fast and kick hard. You can read about how to train to maintain flexibility of these muscles on page 46.

The muscles pass two joints, the hip and the knee. This means that from one end position (stretched hip and bent leg) to the other end position (bent hip and stretched leg) there is a difference of about 20–30 cm. The muscle must therefore be capable of contracting or expanding that much in a very short space of time. This requires suppleness, strength and coordination. The muscles which extend over two joints are exposed to injury far more often than those connected to one. If you have not warmed up, or have become tired, they are easily injured.

Figure 28

Figure 29

Figure 30

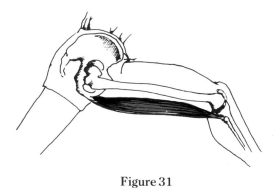

Figure 31

The buttock muscles

The buttock muscles (**Figure 32**) situated at the outside of the hip, are able to lift the leg outwards. They are involved in every step you take. When you put your foot down these muscles are activated and they contract to prevent wavering at the hip joint; for example, the weight of the upper part of the body would make it collapse according to arrow A (**Figure 33**) when landing on your left foot. In this case, the buttock muscles hold up the weight according to arrow B (**Figure 33**). These muscles work hard when one jumps on one leg, runs downhill or changes direction while running, e.g. when dribbling.

Figure 32

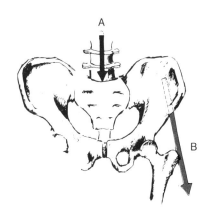

Figure 33

The groin muscles

The groin muscles, which are on the inside of the thigh (**Figure 34**), are responsible for braking the forward swing of the front leg when you are running. When you run forwards, the leg moves straight forward in relation to the ground. If you look at how the leg moves *in relation to the hip joint* (**Figure 35**) it also *swings outwards*. The groin mus-cles pull in the back leg towards the centre when the leg begins the forward swing. The muscles are under particular stress when taking long steps, when stretching the foot forward to reach the ball and when preparing to take a kick (**Figures 36** and **37**).

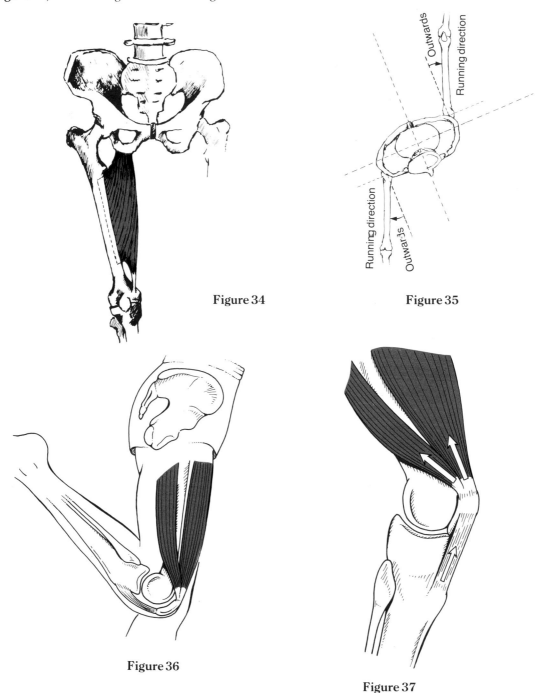

Figure 34

Figure 35

Figure 36

Figure 37

Above all, the strength in the three vastus muscles is absolutely decisive for your ability to kick hard and jump high. All three muscles are attached to the kneecap, which in turn is attached to the upper part of the edge of the tibia via a strong tendon (**Figure 38**). The thicker each muscle is, the greater the force it can contract with and the greater the acceleration which can be transmitted to the lower leg. Altogether, the muscle contracts 5 to 8 cm, which means that the tensile force in the kneecap tendon forces the lower leg forward at ever-higher speed. The connection is simple: twice the muscle thickness = twice the force = twice the acceleration = twice the final speed for the foot = twice as hard a kick. One way of measuring the 'strength' of the muscle group is by measuring the circumference of the thigh 8 cm above the kneecap, with the muscles tensed. It can be particularly important to measure the circumference after injury when the player has been forced to take a lengthy break from training. The injured leg has often shrunk in circumference and the player would be wise to do body-building training until both legs have the same strength (circumference).

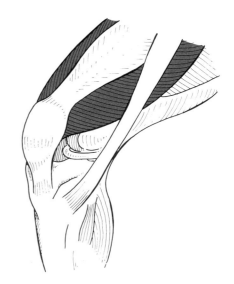

Figure 38

The back muscles and stomach muscles

Figure 39 shows the location of the back muscles and the stomach muscles relative to the vertebrae. The back muscles are thicker and, hence, stronger. The stomach muscles are weaker but are located further away from the vertebrae and therefore have better leverage. The relationship can be compared to two people of different weight sitting on a seesaw (**Figure 40**). To carry out movements of the spine there must be a balance between the back and the stomach muscles. If one muscle group can get the thorax moving the other muscle group must be able to put the brake on before you overstretch and reach positions where the risk of injury increases dramatically.

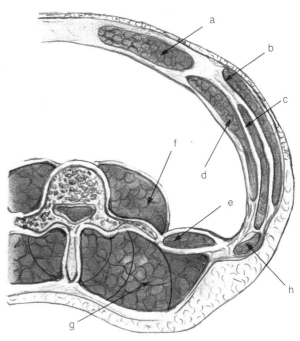

(a) Straight abdominal muscle (rectus abdominis)
(b) External oblique abdominal muscle
(c) Internal oblique abdominal muscle
(d) Transverse abdominal muscle
(e) Square lumbar muscle (quadratus lumborum)
(f) Iliopsoas
(g) Back extensors (erector spinae)
(h) Broad back muscle (latissimus dorsi)

Figure 39

Figure 40

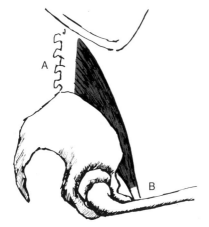

Figure 41 If the back sways 1 to 2 cm at A (i.e. a little) the movement in the leg is reduced by 1 to 2 cm at B.

Figure 42

Stability

The stomach muscles are very important for stabilising the spine when you run, kick and jump. The connection between running fast (or kicking hard) and strong stomach muscles can be seen in **Figure 41**.

The iliopsoas (see **Figure 17**) pulls the thigh forward in running and kicking. It also pulls with exactly the same force on the spine. If the back follows—say 1 to 2 cm—the movement in the thigh will be reduced by 1 to 2 cm. This means 10–20° less swing for the leg; in other words, a much slower movement.

Balance between the back and the stomach muscles

It is the stomach muscles, **Figure 42**, which have to be tensed quickly to prevent movement in the spine. If you have weak untrained stomach muscles you cannot run fast, kick hard, etc., and you will also easily get backache when you run. In order to function well there must be a certain degree of balance in the strength of the back and stomach muscles. Most people are too weak in their stomach in relation to their back, and stomach muscle training is therefore very important. Running at varying speeds, hopping and sideways jumping are very good training, even for back and stomach muscles that are already well trained. But for the purpose of initial training, you can start with normal back and stomach exercises.

KICKING

Try a few kicks without a run-up: stand on one leg and place a ball so that you can kick it as hard as possible with the other leg. Try this exercise a few times and find out which muscles are preventing you from extending the movement as much as you would like.

Muscles which work in kicking

I would guess that you would want to be more elastic in the groin muscles, the knee extensors and perhaps even in the hip flexors, see **Figure 43**.

Flexibility in the groin muscles and the hip flexors

Assume that a movement of 50° is necessary for the thigh bone (the hip flexor performs the work) and 135° for the knee extensors to gain full speed before the foot hits the ball. This means, in **Figure 44**, that you can kick the ball with maximum force just in front of the standing foot—i.e. a hard kick

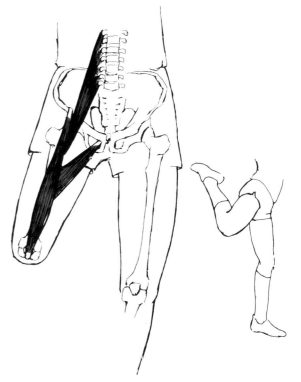

Figure 43

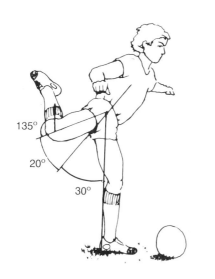

Figure 44

Figure 45

just above the ground. But if you start the kick as in **Figure 45** you will not be able to kick as hard as in **Figure 44** and you will not have full speed until you are in a position where kicking directs the ball upwards. Maybe you can kick pretty hard but the kick will unfortunately be too high. To be able to reach the correct position (**Figure 44**) you have to be flexible in the groins (corresponds to 30° of the whole movement in the picture) and in the hip flexors (corresponds to 20° in the picture).

To be able to kick well you must have:

- *A good technique:* This you will acquire by training to kick in various situations. The aim of the training must be to create as many different situations as possible; for example, this could mean kicking a dead ball or half-volleying or volleying balls crossed from the sides. A good technique is made even better by being flexible enough; that is, if you are able to adjust the position of your body and thereby get a better control of the ball. A stiff player stands less chance of hitting the ball properly if it does not come at exactly the right spot.
- *Flexibility:* You need good flexibility to be able to kick well. Flexibility training by stretching is absolutely necessary in today's football—it does more than just reduce the number of injuries.
- *Strength:* The stronger you are, the harder you can kick. One condition, though, is that your strength training should not make you too stiff. When kicking hard you have probably noticed that your upper body is simultaneously bent

forward. This is because the muscle that swings your leg forward (the hip flexor, **Figure 17**) also bends your spine forward. The harder you kick the more your upper body and arms will rotate in the opposite direction in order to keep you balanced. In other words, you also need an agile upper body to be able to kick hard and maintain your balance.

The word agile may need an explanation. By agile we mean fast, strong and flexible. If you can quickly crawl under a bench, get up on your feet, jump over the bench and crawl under it again, and so on, you are agile. Accordingly, an agile upper body demands a strong back and abdomen and flexibility of the back and hips. You cannot kick really hard or with good accuracy if your upper body is not agile. A football player, therefore, needs to do the warming-up exercises described on page 35.

To kick with maximum force requires perfect coordination among all the major muscle groups in the body and joints, from the elbow joint to the ankle. The prerequisites for a hard kick are for the foot to be travelling at speed, for the foot to meet the ball in the right place and at the right angle and also for the foot to be tensed hard.

A foot that is tensed hard means that the contact between the ball and the foot takes place on a part of the foot that does not crumple in the face of the strong forces present at the moment of contact. An instep stretched by the calf muscles is the best position for the foot.

If you consider that the knee is the fulcrum

around which the lower leg pivots forward, you can see that if you hit with the lower shin (A) the speed will be less than if you hit with point B in the middle of the ankle (**Figure 46**). Point D moves fastest of all but contact here would make the foot give way and the force would be low. The best point of contact is C; that is, 4–5cm below the centre of the ankle joint on the front of the instep.

The foot's point of contact (C) should, on contact with the ball, be on its way straight towards the centre of the ball and in the direction you are going to kick (**Figure 47**). If the force (the direction of movement of the foot) is directed beside the ball's centre the ball will take off more slowly but with spin. The further from the centre the force is directed the more rotation (and less speed) the ball will have. A spin always steals the ball's initial speed. The spin may then be called topspin, underspin, sidespin, etc., depending on which side of the centre of the ball the force is directed.

The speed of the foot is dependent on:

- Maximum bending of the knee, so that the knee extensors are able to exploit their pulling power for as long a stretch as possible.
- The thigh bone being swung as far back as possible and as far outwards as possible (abducted) so that the hip flexors (iliopsoas) and the groin muscles (adductors) are exploited to their utmost.

- The supporting leg being rotated so far out that the pelvis can be turned in towards the supporting leg and hence contribute extra speed to the kicking leg.
- The supporting foot being placed so far to the side of the ball that the distance from the supporting leg hip joint to the ball allows the player maximum stretch in the ankle and knee joints of the kicking leg (**Figure 48**).
- The arms being quite straight and far out from the body and being 'thrown' powerfully in the opposite direction to the movement of the kicking leg. Note that two arms weigh about the same as one leg and are used as a counterweight to the leg. The counter-movement of the arms means that the upper part of the body can be kept more still at the moment of kicking, which gives more impetus to the leg and also better balance and, hence, greater precision (**Figures 49** and **50**). Try kicking with your arms positioned behind your back—you soon realise that you kick not just with your legs but also, to a great degree, with your arms.

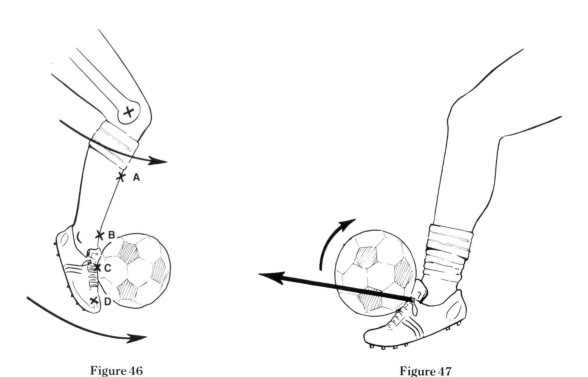

Figure 46   Figure 47

Figure 48

Figure 49   Figure 50

HEADING

Jumping up to head the ball relies on good back and stomach muscles. The head moves with a strong forward flexing of the spine at the same time as the hips are flexed. In order to be able to do this you must first have bent your back backwards and stretched your hips thoroughly.

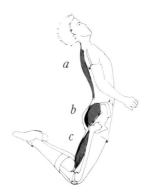

Figure 51

Jumping for a header

The muscles responsible for this action are the back muscles (**Figure 51**(a)), the pelvic muscles (**Figure 51** (b)) and the hamstrings (**Figure 51** (c)). The hamstrings, or 'knee flexors', actually stretch the hips as much as they bend the knees; the effect of using these to stretch backwards from the hips is that you bend the knees. If you do not stretch the hips properly the knees will not bend. In order to be able to build up to the kick properly the corresponding muscles on the front of the body must be long enough to follow through the movement and be stretched to about 20% beyond their resting length. These muscles, namely the stomach muscles (**Figure 52** (a)), the hip flexors (**Figure 52** (b)) and the knee extensors (**Figure 52** (c)), can impart considerable speed to the upper part of the body, and hence to the head, after they have been drawn apart. To execute that kind of header it is important to have strong neck muscles. To direct the header to one side requires mobility in the spine, and strength, above all, in the oblique stomach muscles.

Figure 52

Heading from a standing position

When you head the ball and have both feet on the ground you generally keep your arms somewhat bent and at face level. Then, just before you are about to head the ball, you can pull your arms towards you and give forward speed to your upper body. The muscles that pull your arms towards your body (**Figure 53**), the flexors of the elbow and the broad back muscle, also pull your body forward. Consequently, your head will get some extra speed.

If you have made a jump to reach the ball you can also pull your arms towards you to give extra speed to your head. But if you want to reach as high as possible in an attempt to head the ball your arms and legs should hang vertically the moment the ball is hit.

Figure 53

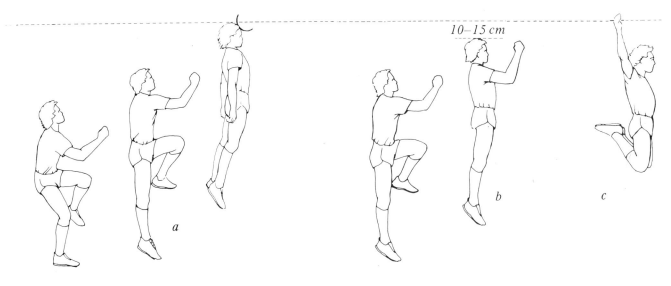

Figure 54. (a) A good position for reaching as high as possible. (b) A good position for making a powerful header. Your legs should be straight the moment the ball is headed. (c) Dangerous position.

Figure 54 shows that your head can reach 10–15 cm higher in a jump if your body is quite straight compared with if you lift your arms and, still more, if you bend your knees. To get as high as possible you, naturally, need to make a good take-off. That means, see **Figure 54** ((a) and (b)), swinging your arms up and forward in front of your chest. Having left the ground, you can then pull your arms down to your sides in order to gain some extra height. Do not adopt the position shown in **Figure 54(c)** which is potentially dangerous and can result in injury.

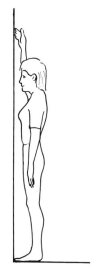

Figure 55

Techniques for the take-off

A take-off from a standing position is preferably executed with both feet on the ground. You swing your arms up and in front of your chest, bend your knees a bit, not too deep and not too fast, and make your jump with both your legs engaged at the same time. This type of hop, known as a 'sergeant jump', is often used to measure a person's power. Stand next to a wall and try to reach as high up as you can with the fingertips of one hand (**Figure 55**), or stand under a high-jump bar, placed so that you can just reach it. Then, jump up repeatedly, measuring how far up the wall you can reach, or raise the bar until you cannot jump up and touch it. The athletes who get the best results in this type of measurement are volleyball players (good technique) and weightlifters (great strength in their legs). Results of up to 90 cm are not uncommon. How high can you lift your body in a sergeant jump? How high is the average in your team? Train extra hard with the different jumping exercises for 6–8 weeks and measure again to see if you and the team have improved your results.

If you have to move one step before the take-off we call it a one-step run-up. Then, there are two possibilities: either you make the jump with one leg or you put your other foot close to your standing foot and make the jump with both legs. You swing your arms in the same ways regardless of what type of jump you choose to make. Volleyball players learn a pattern of movements that enables them to jump high with good balance by jumping off both feet with a three-step run-up. It feels a little unnatural and is difficult to begin with, but produces advantages if you have practised it. If you take more than a three-step run-up, your speed becomes so great that it is more worthwhile to jump from one foot. You use the speed and counterbalance it with a relatively straight leg. Use a high-jump bar to find out how high you can jump on your best leg and on your worst. Do exercises which make you jump up from the left and the right leg alternately. In football matches you will often find yourself in situations where you can choose how you are going to jump. So learn how you can jump highest in different situations and take the option which suits you best in each situation.

POWER

What do we mean when we say that a player is powerful? Most of us probably put an equals sign between power and jumping high. The higher you can jump the more powerful you are. We can add to the equation; including, for example, starting speed and ability to change direction quickly and to stop quickly, which are factors in being explosively strong. Accordingly, being powerful demands explosive strength, a good balance and coordination.

The large buttock muscle and the calf muscle

The muscle that works hard at starts, accelerations and jumps is the hip extensor (the large buttock muscle; **Figure 56**). All powerful backward drives of the leg are performed with the hip bent, so that the buttock muscle is drawn out and charged. You start the backward drive just after the muscle has been drawn out.

The calf muscle (**Figure 57**) is responsible for a large part of the power when you are running. It is engaged late in the backward drive of the leg, late enough for the leg to be almost straight before you start straightening the ankle. If you look at how the muscle is inserted, you understand that this muscle is also drawn out before it starts working powerfully. Consequently, you straighten your knee in order to draw out your calf muscle. When starting from a standing position you lean a great deal forward. If you do not have ankle joints that are flexible enough, you can angle out your feet a little, i.e. run Chaplin-like for the first 3–4 steps.

Thus, in the beginning you obtain power from the hip and knee extensors; but, having gained speed, the calf muscle then plays a more important role.

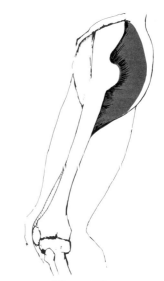

Figure 56

Figure 57

Power training

As far as power training is concerned, there are many different theories, but what is known is that:

- A muscle can develop up to 40% more power if it is made to put a brake on the body compared with when the same muscle is used to get the body moving. In other words, you are at least 40% stronger in landing than in jumping up; you are 40% stronger when you lower yourself from hanging by a bent arm than when you pull yourself up; you are 40% stronger when you bend your arm in a press-up than when you stretch your arm to come up again.
- A muscle grows and gets stronger if it is exposed to strong forces. This means that you can do bodybuilding training by, for example, squatting immediately followed by jumping up. You are thus making the muscle brake with maximum force before it executes the jumping up, which is what you are actually interested in. This type of training is sometimes called negative bodybuilding. The word negative is used because you reduce the body's speed before subsequently accelerating. In practical terms this means that you can train to enhance your strength/power by doing a series of jumps; for example:

- high jumps off one leg 3–4 times
- long jumps off one leg 3–4 times
- running with 6–8 long strides at high speed
- high jumps 3–4 times off both feet
- long jumps 3–4 times off both feet
- 1 step run-up—bring other foot up and jump up from both feet
- 1 step run-up and jump up from one foot
- 2–4 step run-up and jump up from one foot

All these exercises can and indeed, preferably, should be carried out with a ball. A few players should work together in a small group so that on your last jump a ball is thrown up to you and you have to head it back. Then take the ball yourself and throw it up for the next player.

Do not do more than 4 jumps per leg before concluding the jump sequence with, e.g. a header, or just by turning and jogging back for a new jump sequence. So it is better to do 4 maximum jumps than 8–10 halfway jumps. Building up your strength requires maximum effort.

Being powerful also means being able to brake and being able to change direction quickly. Working in pairs, for instance, one player runs in a figure of eight around two cones and each circuit is forced to jump up and send a header back to the other player who throws in a header pass, as in **Figure 58**.

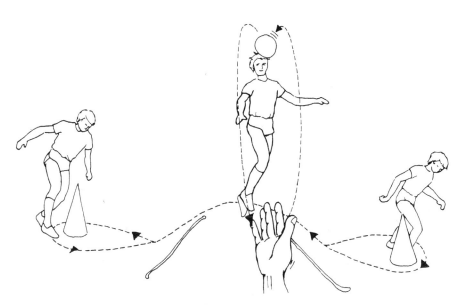

Figure 58

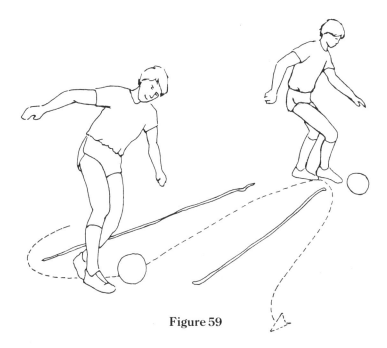

Figure 59

With the help of a skipping rope laid out on the ground you can arrange lots of variations on the jumping/dribbling/heading exercises. You can hop on one leg in every square, jump over alternate squares, dribble round the rope, etc., **Figure 59**.

An effective method of training is to use some boxes of a suitable height to jump down from, in order to increase the strain to which the muscle is exposed on braking. This 'negative training' is also called eccentric training. The word eccentric is used because the muscle is working and trying to stop movement in the joint; thus the muscle is trying to contract while outer forces are making it expand. Place the boxes as shown in **Figure 60** and do 4–5 jumps, jumping up and down on the right leg only. Next, carry out the same exercise, using the left leg. Then, the third time, jump with both feet. This method of training places a lot of strain on your body and must not be too intensive. Be aware of any tenderness in the kneecap tendons, the Achilles tendons or the hip muscles. Tenderness is a sign of strain and should lead to a reduction in the training.

Speed

Most people probably equate 'speed' with running a fast 100 metres. A person who is fast over short distances, e.g. is leading a 100 metre race after 10 metres and, perhaps, even after 20 metres, but is last to finish, has the type of speed which is suitable for football. This kind of quick-start player is probably powerful too. Power training thus also produces a speed which can be used precisely for football.

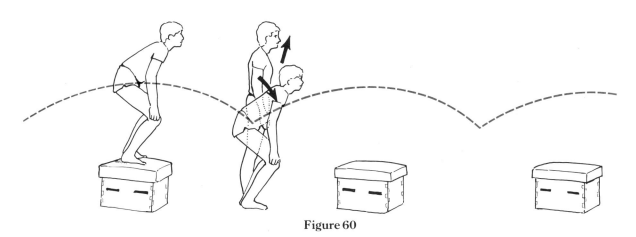

Figure 60

4 Knees and Feet

Knees and feet are exposed to severe stresses and are injured relatively often in football. We now describe the structure of the knee and the ankle joints to further your understanding of how and why you should do bodybuilding or agility training for the muscles that surround these joints. Increased knowledge produces better training and, therefore, reduces the number of injuries; at the same time, this training will increase your speed and power.

THE KNEE JOINT

The knee joint works as follows: the lower end of the thigh bone (femur) is formed of two egg-shaped surfaces (condyles) that rest on the two flat surfaces on the top end of the shin bone (tibia). The bones are joined together by ligaments (bands of connective tissue) on the inside and outside of the leg (**Figure 61a, b**). These ligaments prevent sideways movements (wobbling), without preventing bending and stretching in the knee. When you bend the knee, the side ligaments are not taut but allow a certain degree of turning in the lower leg relative to the thigh. The rotation is stopped when the lateral ligament is stretched to its fullest extent. If there is a violent twist, the ligament can tear.

In the gap between the egg-shaped condyles of the thigh bone, two ligaments grow out and extend to the middle of the shin bone. These ligaments are called the anterior and posterior cruciate ligaments (**Figure 61c**). The anterior cruciate ligament prevents the lower leg from slipping forward relative to the thigh bone. The posterior cruciate ligament prevents backwards slipping and overstretching. Together, they also prevent the lower leg from rotating too far inwards. When the effects of a movement are excessive, e.g. kicks which miss, kicking the ground or when the studs get stuck in the ground and you twist your thorax, one or more of these ligaments may be damaged. The best protection against this is strong muscles that can brake the movement and prevent overstretching.

Strong muscles are always the best protection against injuries. The hamstring muscles prevent overstretching and excessive rotation of the lower leg. The extensor musculature of the knee prevents excessively deep knee-bends, with their risk of injury.

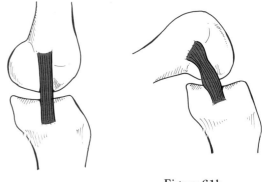

Figure 61a

Figure 61b

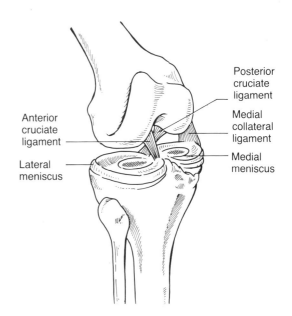

Posterior cruciate ligament

Medial collateral ligament

Medial meniscus

Anterior cruciate ligament

Lateral meniscus

Figure 61c

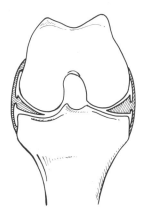

Figure 62a

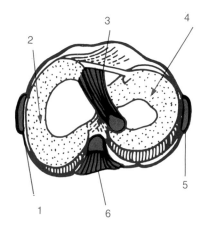

1. Medial collateral ligament
2. Medial meniscus
3. Anterior cruciate
4. Lateral meniscus
5. Lateral collateral ligament
6. Posterior cruciate ligament

Figure 62b

The egg-shaped surfaces of the thigh bone are covered with cartilage and rest on the equally cartilaginous flat surfaces of the shin bone. Regardless of the 'elastic cartilage', both support surfaces that are too small (about the size of a small coin) to prevent wear on the knee joint cartilage. The surfaces are extended by two 'inserts', which look like orange segments. These are bowl-shaped (concave) on top, i.e. they match the egg-shaped surfaces of the thigh bone, and flat underneath, i.e. they match the flat top of the shin bone.

These inserts are called the menisci (**Figures 61c, 62a, b**) and they are attached by means of short tendons to the lower leg, between the two cartilage-covered surfaces; the total wear surface in the knee joint is increased 3 to 4 times what it would have been without any menisci. The medial meniscus is also attached to the inner collateral

ligament, which means that it is not so easy for it to move and adjust to movements which take place in the knee. As a result the medial meniscus is injured far more often than the lateral one. About 8 out of 10 injuries affect the inner collateral ligament. Injuries most often occur when the knee is bending at the same time as the lower leg is rotating outwards. Walking, running or hopping in a low crouching position are exercises that are often used for football. These exercises may be actually damaging and should be avoided. Exercises to strengthen the muscles which go round the knee joint and thus protect the knee from injury are described both in the stretching section (page 43) and in the strength training section (page 57).

THE ANKLE JOINT

The foot is a very complex structure that consists of 26 separate bones. The bones at the back of the foot, together with the shin bone, form two joints where the major movements of the foot have their impact. Between the tibia (shin bone) and the talus (ankle bone) bending and stretching occur. The large muscle group that enables us to stretch our ankles, rise up on our toes, jump up, etc., is called the calf muscle (triceps surae). There are other muscles that lift the foot in the opposite direction; for example they enable you to walk on your heels without putting the front part of your foot on the ground. They are called the tibialis anterior (front

shin bone muscle), the extensor hallucis longus (long big toe extensor) and the extensor digitorum longus (long toe extensor).

The foot can also be tilted sideways. The positions are called pronation (when the little toe side of the foot is raised from the floor) and supination (when the big toe side is raised from the floor); **Figure 63** shows the different directions of movement of the foot. On the outside of the foot, slightly in front of and below the malleolus (the lower tip of the fibula) you can feel the two tendons which belong to the fibular muscles (fibularis longus and brevis). These muscles tilt the foot from a supine to a prone position. On the inside of the ankle joint there are three tendons which tilt the foot from the prone to the supine position.

When running at a moderate speed you put your foot down so that the outside of the heel touches the ground first. You say that the foot is extended and supine. In the course of that step your weight is transferred forwards and inwards. The foot leaves the ground flexed and prone; in other words, you push off with your foot from the big toe side. If you look at the skeleton of the foot, you realise that this action is putting most of the strain on the larger bones of the foot (**Figures 64(a)** and **64(b)**). The bones which run along this slightly S-shaped curve form part of the foot's 'support arch'.

On the inside of the foot the bones are constructed like the arch of a bridge and the structure is called the 'movement arch'. The movement arch is supported not only by the shape of the bones but also by muscles which come from the lower leg. When you land on your foot in a running step the greatest force of the impact is absorbed towards the heel bone. On the other hand, if you place your whole foot on the ground, the instep (movement arch) bends downwards and the muscle is exposed to a tug which produces stresses in the area of the muscle root. Too much landing on hard ground with the wrong foot position and perhaps also with poorly constructed shoes can easily produce strain injuries. These injuries are called periostitis and they feel like aches in the lower leg. They occur precisely when you are running or after a training session. Take these symptoms seriously and ask your sports doctor what you should do. Otherwise, the risk of a chronic condition setting in is great.

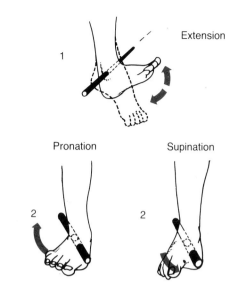

Figure 63 The foot can move around two axes. Movements around axis 1 are called flexion and extension. Movements around axis 2 are called supination and pronation.

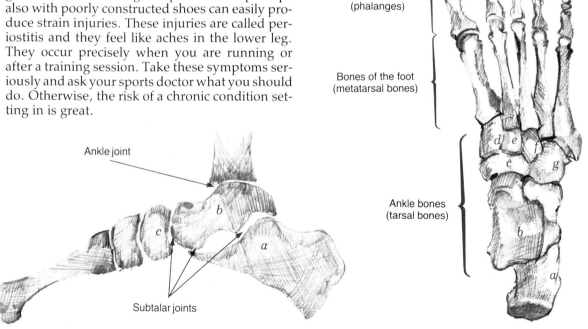

Ankle joint

Subtalar joints

Figure 64b

Bones of the toe (phalanges)

Bones of the foot (metatarsal bones)

Ankle bones (tarsal bones)

Figure 64a

Ankle bones

a Heel bone (calcaneus)
b Ankle bone (talus)
c Boat-shaped tarsal bone (navicular)
d, e, f Wedge-shaped bones (cuneiforms)
g Cube-shaped bone (cuboid)

Excessive movement in pronation and supination can be prevented, as always, by strong muscles and ligaments. The most important ligaments that protect the foot grow out from the tips of the tibia and fibula. They are attached to different parts of the rear bones of the foot. On the outside of the foot there are three different ligaments and on the inside there is a triangular ligament (**Figures 65(a), (b)**). With injuries that produce severe pain and swelling you should always consult a doctor.

Figure 65a

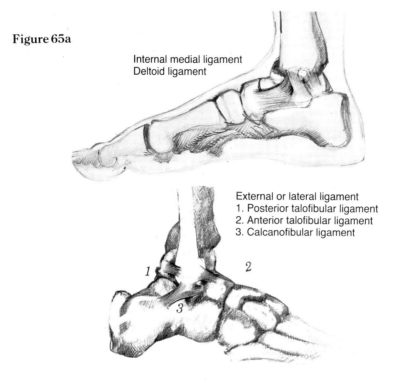

Internal medial ligament
Deltoid ligament

External or lateral ligament
1. Posterior talofibular ligament
2. Anterior talofibular ligament
3. Calcanofibular ligament

Figure 65b

5 Warming-up

In all sports activities be strict about warming-up and limbering-up. It is very important to warm-up before hard work. Although it is increasingly important the older you become, younger players also have to warm-up properly in order to reduce the risk of injury. As the muscle warms, the nerve impulses travel faster and the body reacts quicker. By proper warming-up you can avoid injuries such as sprained ankles and ruptured muscles. The warmer you are, the more easily the various muscles will glide against each other; this makes your movements quicker and more precise. An inactive muscle has a low blood supply and a fairly low temperature (between 35 and 36°C, depending on what muscle you measure). For an active muscle to function perfectly it should have a temperature of 38°C. It takes about 10–15 min of intensive activity before your whole body reaches this temperature. The best way of warming-up is to move so that your large muscles have to work. Accordingly, you should run, jump, swing your arms, make elastic stretchings, etc. We distinguish between warming-up, which aims at raising the temperature of muscles, and limbering-up, which aims at stressing joints, muscles, tendons, etc. The warming-up gradually passes on to limbering-up. Start by jogging and gradually pass on to short rushes, high knee liftings, backward heel kicks and, finally, finish with strenuous exercises such as jumping on one leg and jumping with both feet together. Preferably, you should do all this in types of exercises where you train technique with the ball at the same time.

WARMING-UP PROGRAMME

Here is a programme for warming-up. You should jog, run and jump to get warm. Since this takes at least 10 min you have to spend the time well by practising passes, receiving passes, heading and dribbling at the same time. When you do not have the ball, do exercises that make you more elastic, faster and flexible. Move to and fro across the ground and vary the type of pass you make every time you move and the kind of exercise you do when you do not have the ball.

The curve in **Figure 66** shows the rise in temperature inside the extensor muscle of the thigh when the subject of the experiment jogged with relatively high intensity. It took nine minutes to become warm enough (about 38°C). When the subject rested, the temperature quickly dropped back to below the level which is acceptable when one is going to expose the body to sudden runs, high jumps, kicks, etc.

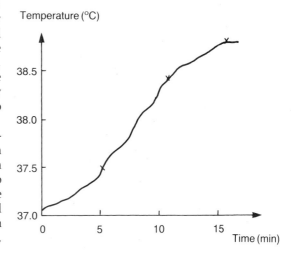

Figure 66

Stage 1

Divide yourselves up into groups of 4 players (if necessary 3), **Figure 67**. Jog from one side of the pitch to the other and back again, playing the ball to each other the whole time.

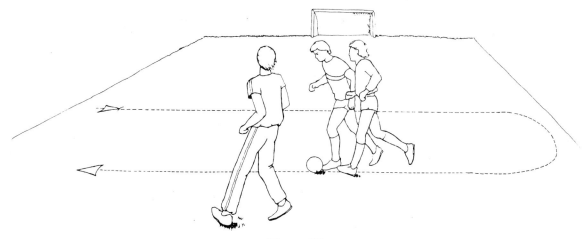

Figure 67

Stage 2

Run the same stretch again but sideways this time, **Figure 68**. You can run as you like when you are receiving a pass and when you are passing the ball on.

Figure 68

Stage 3

Run across the field again while passing to each other. Run so that you kick your buttocks when you don't have the ball. On the way back, run pulling your knees up high, **Figure 69**.

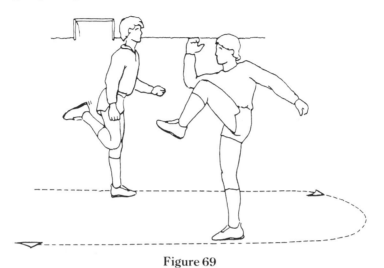

Figure 69

Stage 4

Cross the same stretch again, but this time jumping rather than running, **Figure 70**. Vary it so that you sometimes jump from your left leg, sometimes from your right and sometimes from both feet. Pass the ball so that it is received on the chest or the head. Bring it down and then pass it again with normal steps. When you have got rid of the ball, jump again.

Figure 70

With a little imagination you and your teammates, together with your coach, can invent a fun new exercise at each training session so that the warming-up becomes effective and challenging too.

6 Limbering-up

After completing the four stages of warming-up as detailed in Chapter 5, you should be ready for the limbering-up stage. You must now do some exercises without the ball in order to be able to maintain high intensity and to be able to concentrate on maximum explosivity; for example, jumping and changing direction. In other exercises, it is best to include the ball.

LIMBERING-UP PROGRAMME

Stage 1

Place yourselves about 2 metres apart, **Figure 71**. Drop forwards and do a few press-ups. The last player jumps with feet together over the others. When someone has jumped over you, you get up and jump over your three companions yourself. Drop down quickly and begin working on the press-ups again. Travel from one sideline to the other.

Figure 71

Stage 2

On the way back, drop forward and hop forward with the left and right feet alternately; the forward foot must not touch the ground, **Figure 72**. The last player runs a 'slalom course' between the rest of you. When he or she has dropped down in front, the next player weaves in and out, and so on.

Figure 72

Stage 3

The same pattern as before; that is, 3 players working and 1 running, **Figure** 73. Travel one width of the field. This time the players who are on the ground should support themselves on their arms, but with their faces and stomachs facing up. Hop so that you are only supported on one leg at a time. The leg which is in the air should be stretched fully each time. The player who is running should run sideways and jump with both feet together over the one on the ground. Think up some variations of your own. Keep going for at least 5 min in total.

In the next section you can read about agility in a little more detail, but here it should be pointed out that stretching exercises are particularly important to footballers. During limbering-up you should make sure that you always spend a few minutes on exercises of this type, **Figures 74–78**.

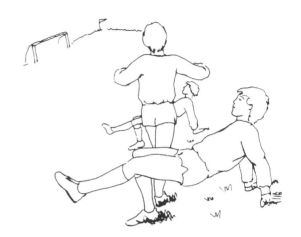

Figure 73

74   75   76

Figures 74–78

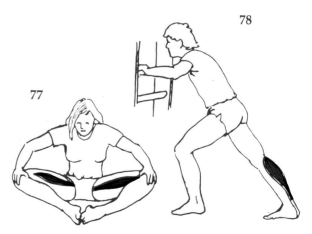

78

77

40

PREPARATION = WARMING-UP + LIMBERING-UP + STRETCHING

Young players

The younger you are the smaller is the physiological need for preparation. Preparation is important, however, for other reasons. It helps concentration and control and strengthens the team morale. For younger players 5 min should be enough before training. During this period, you should mainly exercise with the ball. The tempo of training should be gradually increased for rather tough play situations after 10–15 min. You should be able to take care of your own warming-up before a match. It may not be possible to warm-up together on a ground. Therefore, you have to know a number of exercises that warm and limber you up and also have a stretching effect on your muscles. If you are well prepared you can manage to start a match at a high tempo from the beginning.

14–15 year olds

By the age of 14–15 the demands on you to limber-up and stretch become greater: 10 min preparation will then be a minimum demand. Mix ball exercises with other exercises during the warming-up programme. On the whole you should try to warm yourself playing with a ball. Stretching exercises are necessary for you to avoid injuries and become faster and more elastic, but these should come after sufficient warming-up and limbering-up. Stretching does not replace good warming-up—it is a good complement.

Older players

The older you are the more important it is to prepare yourself. For older players, preparation for 15 min, perhaps including 5 min stretching, is absolutely essential. Stretching exercises should be done between limbering-up exercises so that you do not get cold during the stretching. This is because stretching itself gives only a slight addition of warmth to a muscle and only to the particular muscle that you are stretching.

Note that it is just as important to stretch after training or after a match as before. Investigations show that stiffness and shortening of muscles last for days after hard work. By stretching it is possible to maintain and even increase your flexibility.

7 Flexibility Training

In this chapter we begin by explaining why you should try to increase your flexibility (agility) and how to do it. When we were analysing how your muscles were engaged while running, kicking, and so on, we came to the conclusion that it was important to have flexible muscles in the groin, at the front and back of the thigh, a flexible iliopsoas, i.e. the muscle that flexes the hip and, finally, elastic calf muscles (see pages 15–24).

The leg muscles

The knee extensors, **Figure 79**, must be long enough for you to bend your lower leg up well when you are running fast or kicking hard ground kicks. The knee flexors, **Figure 80**, must be long enough to avoid being ruptured after you have kicked, as they end up in a rather exposed position after the kick.

The hip flexors, **Figure 81**, help determine how far back you can swing your leg. This is important, above all, when making contact with a dead ball. If you are trying to shoot hard and, at the same time, keep the ball down, your leg must start from a position where it is properly swung back, with the heel almost touching your buttocks, in order for your foot to gain enough speed before the strike. The length of your calf muscle determines your starting speed. If you have a stiff ankle joint it is difficult to lean forward enough at the start. The knee extensors, knee flexors and hip flexors will also avoid injuries easier if they are not too short. **Figures 79–81** show how you can stretch them: we will return to stretching later. On page 11–12 you can see better how the muscles are attached to the skeleton.

The muscle comprises connective tissue and muscle cells. The connective tissue is found as a casing around the whole muscle and as bands running through it, dividing the muscle into different sub-sections. Bundles of muscle cells are surrounded by thinner connective tissue and each individual cell is surrounded by very elastic connective tissue. All these bands of connective tissue run together at both ends of the muscle and form tendons. The muscle cell is very elastic and does not prevent a muscle being extended, whereas the bands of connective tissue are very resistant to sudden tugs and strong traction and prevent the muscle being overextended. When you stretch, make sure that the muscle cells are completely at rest (the muscle is relaxed) and that for a relatively long time, 10–30 seconds, you pull on both the tendons of the muscle and, thus, on the connective tissue which runs through the muscle. Sudden sharp stretches have no effect at all, but moderate force for a long time makes the connective tissue give a little. The muscle becomes a fraction longer.

Figure 79

Figure 80

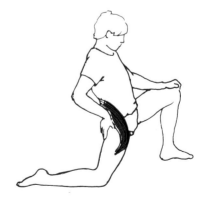

Figure 81

THE CONTRACTION–RELAXATION–STRETCHING METHOD

To lengthen a muscle effectively use the contraction–relaxation–stretching method. Stand in a position where the muscle you wish to stretch is maximally drawn out. **Figure 82** shows a way of stretching your knee extensor (compare **Figure 7**). In this position try to straighten your knee at the same time as you are preventing it by holding the leg tightly with your hand. Let your knee extensor go at it vigorously for about 6 seconds. Then relax for 2 seconds. Not until now does the real stretching of the muscle begin. This is done during a period of 10 seconds by gently pulling your leg backwards 2 cm with your hand until you feel that your muscle is drawn out at the front of your thigh. After 10 seconds start again by trying to straighten your knee for 6 seconds, relaxing for 2 seconds and then stretching gently for another 10 seconds. Repeat the procedure 3–5 times. This particular method has shown itself to be the best when it comes to getting the desired length of a muscle that is too short. Once you have the length of muscles needed to be a good footballer you must continue training for flexibility but only in order to maintain your acquired flexibility (a flexibility test is described on page 49). Above all, this is important after hard training. You can then utilise stretching.

WHAT IS STRETCHING?

Stretching differs from the contraction–relaxation–stretching method in that you are only trying to draw out a relaxed muscle. Stand like the person in **Figure 82** and pull gently with your hand until you feel that the muscle on the front of your thigh is tight; stand like this for about 30 seconds. Then, shake loose and repeat the procedure once more. The more you subject your muscles to strength training, the more tendency they will have to become shortened. Consequently, stretching is of great importance to all sportsmen, including footballers, who get strong leg muscles through their training. Stretching not only helps prevent injuries but also gives you the ability to run faster and to kick harder. **Figures 83–85** show some positions of each of those muscles whose

Figure 82 A drawn-out knee muscle.

flexibility is important to a footballer. Choose a position for each muscle that suits you personally. Use stretching or the contraction–relaxation–stretching method at least every other day. Be careful to warm-up before starting.

The groin

There are five separate muscles which you can stretch by spreading your legs as much as possible. One of these five muscles passes the knee joint before it is inserted into the shin bone. This means you have to spread your legs with straight knees. Consequently, using the position in **Figure 85** is not enough because then you can still meet with a rupture of your muscle however agile you have become in that position. Accordingly, you should combine the position shown in **Figure 85** with that in **Figure 83** or **Figure 84**. If you use the position in **Figure 84** you can sit with your feet against a wall. Push the insides of your feet against the wall for 6 seconds (you should stop if you feel a pain in the inside of your knee), relax for 2 seconds and then try to spread your legs another few centimetres. Now, sit in this position for 10 seconds. Repeat the procedure 3–5 times.

Figures 83–85

The knee extensors

The position shown in **Figure 86** is the most common and the easiest to use to stretch your knee extensors. In this position it is important that your hips are thrust forward properly. The muscles on the front of your thigh should be tight but you must not feel a pain in your knee. Try kneeling like the person in **Figure 87**, i.e. with your hips thrust forward as far as possible; then, seize your lower leg with your hand and try to pull your heel right up to your buttocks. If you can do that there is no need for further stretching. The positions in **Figures 86** and **88** have, in principle, the same effect.

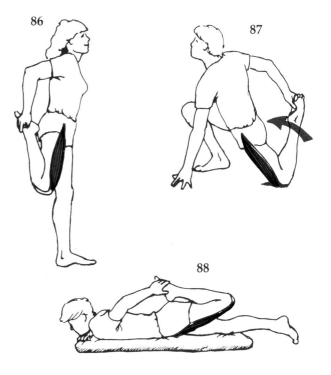

Figures 86–88

Figures 89–91

The pelvic muscles

If you do a lot of running training you may easily experience a pain on the outside of the knee. A common cause is shortened and very tense muscles. This applies above all to the pelvic muscles and to a long tendon band that runs from the pelvic muscles down the outside of the thigh to the outside of the shin bone. After a hard training session you should therefore stretch in one of the positions shown in **Figures 89–91**. You should feel it working; that is, expanding the muscles that pass the outside of the hip joint.

Figure 92

The knee flexors

Figure 92 shows a way of testing flexibility. Stand with bent legs and with your fingertips properly on the ground. Then gently stretch your legs and see if you can straighten them without lifting your fingertips off the ground. The base of your back should not hurt!

Figures 93–95 show different ways of stretching the knee flexors. The exercise in **Figure 93** is the most effective. You can put your heel on the ground, against a stone or on a bench. If you are fairly supple you might need to kneel on your left leg in order to manage to stretch your right leg as in **Figure 94**. You should feel this on the back of your thigh, but not in the small of your back. It is always better to take one leg at a time. In every case you should fall forward from the hips, not by bending your back as in **Figure 96**.

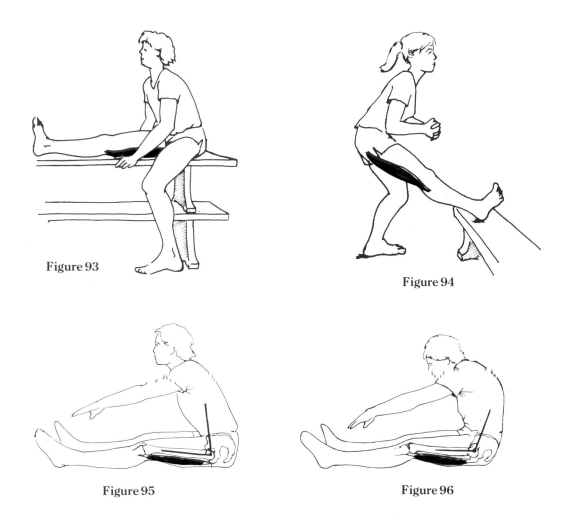

Figure 93

Figure 94

Figure 95

Figure 96

The hip flexors

Although elasticity in the hip joints is important, it is, unfortunately, very difficult to get at the hip flexor. **Figures 97–99** show how you can stretch this muscle; the position in **Figure 97** is perhaps the best. When you have completed the stretching in this, or one of the other positions, it is a good idea to finish with gentle swings and extensions. What happens when you are running or building up to a kick is precisely a quick extension of this muscle before it has to contract and get the leg going.

Figure 97

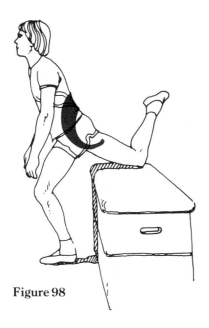

Figure 98

Figure 99

The calf muscle

The calf muscle comprises the gastrocnemius and the soleus. The gastrocnemius passes both the knee joint and the ankle joint (see **Figure 15**) and can therefore be stretched with the exercises in **Figures 100–102**; that is with the knee straight and the foot flexed. The soleus passes only the ankle joint and has to be stretched with the knee bent and the foot flexed, **Figure 103**.

Figure 100

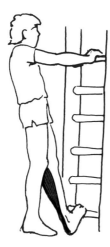

Figure 101

Figure 102

Some advice on stretching

Remember to mix a few stretching exercises in with the limbering-up programme (see page 39). Finish every hard training session and every match with at least one exercise for each group of muscles, as described above. We suggest two exercises for the groin, one exercise for the knee extensors, one for the pelvic muscles, one for the knee flexors, one for the hip flexors and one for the calf muscle.

It is important to choose the position or positions which suit you. If you are 'stiff' some positions will suit you and if you are already fairly elastic you must choose others. Try it and see. In all forms of agility training it is necessary to know that the objective is to achieve a more agile body. The contraction method is excellent for restoring the normal length to a muscle which has become foreshortened (through injury or bad training). When the muscle has returned to its normal length, exercises for suppleness and extensions are a way of 'teaching' the muscle to work properly. After each stretching session you should

Figure 103

therefore do a few exercises in which you swing the leg rhythmically towards whatever positions you want. You may want to end each of the stretching exercises with gentle extensions in the same position.

MEASURING YOUR AGILITY

Before you begin agility training it can be fun to know how stiff or agile you are. You can then see whether your training is producing good results. It can also be useful to know what is acceptable agility, for there is no need to become over-agile.

With the help of a friend and a tape measure you can measure your agility (**Figures 104–108**). There are no ideal values. Compare notes with your friends and make sure you achieve a few centimetres improvement with stretching exercises. Also check that you have the same mobility on both sides of the body. This applies to all mobility training. Different degrees of mobility on different sides always means a greater tendency to injury.

Calf muscles

How far from a wall can you place your foot and still touch the wall with your knee? Bend forward at the ankle as far as you can, **Figure 104**. You should be barefoot or have the same shoes on each time you measure, and the heel must be resting on the ground. Feel the pull on your calf muscle or your Achilles tendon—not in the ankle joint itself. If there is resistance at the back of the lower leg, it is the calf muscle that is the problem and you can improve a few extra centimetres with stretching exercises. If there is resistance at the ankle joint, it is the construction and the ligament of the ankle that are causing the problem and in this case you must not try to increase agility.

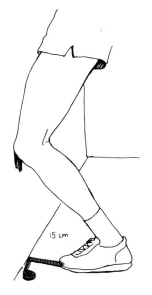

15 cm

Figure 104

It is a good idea to be barefoot when you do this test. A heel on a shoe would mean you would get far too high a reading. However, if you do have shoes on the first time you measure, you should have the same shoes on the next time you test.

The hamstrings

Stand on one leg with a straight knee, with your back against the wall. Someone then lifts the other leg, which must also be kept straight, and measures the distance from the heel to the floor when you cannot get any higher without bending one of your legs (**Figure 105**).

You should be able to get the heel above the horizontal while keeping the leg straight and the back flat against the wall.

The groin

Sit facing a wall, spreading your legs as wide apart as possible. Move as close to the wall as you can, keeping your legs straight. Measure the distance between your heels. You can usually achieve a 90° angle between the legs; that converts to about 140 cm between the heels if your legs are 1 m long (**Figure 106**).

Next, lie on your stomach, bending both feet up towards your buttocks using your hands to help you. Do not twist your hip joint. If your heels do not reach your buttocks, your knee extensors are too stiff. The aim is to be able to lift your knees 10–15 cm from the floor with your heels on your buttocks. In this way you can test both knee extensors and hip flexors. Warm up properly before you measure.

If you have big calf muscles *and* strong muscles on the backs of your thighs, these may prevent you from getting your heels on to your buttocks. You must accept a few minus centimetres in the records in this case (**Figure 107**). You may still be able to lift up your knees from the floor as in **Figure 108** and, in this way, get a few extra centimetres as compensation.

Fill in the results in Table 1, so that you can easily check the effect of your agility training.

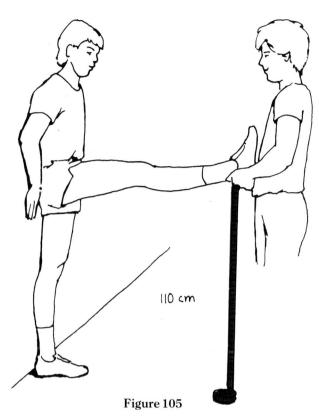

110 cm

Figure 105

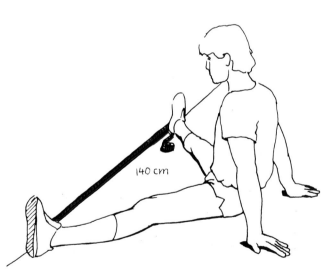

140 cm

Figure 106

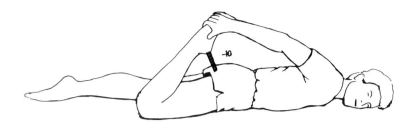

Figure 107

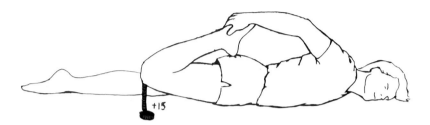

Figure 108

Table 1. Measuring your agility.

	Fig. 104	Fig. 105	Fig. 106	Fig. 107	Fig. 108
First measurement					
After 6 weeks					
After 12 weeks					
After 18 weeks					
After 24 weeks					

8 Strength Training

STRENGTH IN FOOTBALL

A footballer needs strength to be able to run fast, change direction when running, jump high, start quickly and kick hard. You develop this kind of strength by doing specific movements and exercises that force you to run that bit faster and jump that bit higher than you would do in a match. Young people, up to 16 years of age, should combine a great number of various running, jumping and elastic stretching exercises in their training programmes.

If you are 17–18 years old or older, this training can be complemented by training with weights or special equipment. Regardless of what method of training you decide to use, you must not neglect your flexibility training. The more strength training you do, the more flexibility training you need. If you are 15–20 years old you will become stronger automatically, and, correspondingly, a bit stiffer, regardless of the intensity of your training. Therefore, you should take extra care to train your flexibility. Furthermore, you should be aware that the best age for training strength, and thereby building a strong and powerful body, is between 15 and 20. So, strength training is really worthwhile during these years. However, do not deceive yourself into believing that you will become the best player by pumping-up big leg muscles in the gym. The most important thing is to teach your trained and strong muscles to jump, run and change directions.

We now consider the structure and some of the properties of muscles to give you an understanding of how and why they should be trained in certain ways.

ANATOMY OF THE MUSCLE

A muscle (**Figure 109**) consists of bundles of muscle cells, or muscle fibres. The fibre, in turn, is also composed of smaller components, called

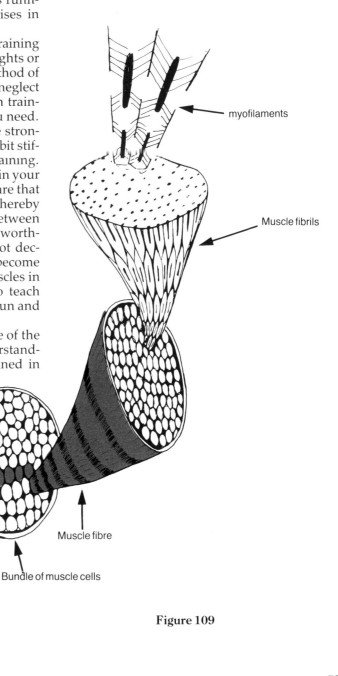

myofilaments

Muscle fibrils

Muscle fibre

Bundle of muscle cells

Muscle

Figure 109

muscle fibrils, which are built up of chains of protein or myofilaments. You are born with a certain number of muscle cells, and this number cannot be changed. However, each cell can become thicker, i.e. contain more chains of protein. By training, you can increase the cross-sectional area of the muscle cell nearly 10 times. The harder you make a muscle work the thicker it will grow in order to manage the stress it is subjected to. A muscle cannot work for more than a few seconds without receiving oxygen from the blood. A muscle that works often and hard for a long time needs a large supply of blood vessels for the muscle cells. The number of vessels (capillaries) supplying the muscles increases if the muscle is regularly subjected to stress.

This type of training, dynamic endurance training, should be executed with light workloads. If you wish to enlarge and strengthen muscles, however, and increase your maximum strength, you should work for shorter periods and use heavy workloads.

PHYSIOLOGICAL PROPERTIES OF THE MUSCLE

Each time a muscle is exposed to a stress that it can only just manage, it reacts by gradually increasing the number of fibrils in the cells exposed to 'overload'. The cells thus thicken, which makes the whole muscle thicker. Increased thickness translates into increased pull. The muscle has become stronger. The pull is transmitted to the different bones which the muscle is attached to via the fasciae and tendons and these too have to become stronger. If you train a muscle with loads which are too heavy, the muscle cells grow relatively quickly but it takes longer for the tendons and ligaments to adjust. Strain injuries may therefore easily result from too much bodybuilding. Always follow a training programme that is adjusted to precisely your requirements. Begin with an introductory period of 4–6 weeks of easy exercises (light weights), which are repeated lots of times. Only then can you increase the load and reduce the number of repetitions. Do not make the mistake of training too ambitiously and hard in the beginning so that you then have to interrupt your training because of minor injuries resulting from strain. Any increased strength that you may have managed to achieve will disappear quite quickly if you have to rest completely from training for some weeks. A rough guide is that with *three* training sessions a week you increase the muscle strength. With *one* training session a week you retain your strength. With no training at all you soon lose the strength of well-trained muscles.

A muscle consists principally of two different types of muscle cell, slow cells and fast cells. The slow cells need oxygen to be able to work and are used when movements do not need so much force or high speed. These cells are best trained by repeating an exercise many times with not too great a load. The result is that these cells become more and more tough and you can repeat the movements more and more times without getting tired. With a heavy load you force the fast cells to work as well and these increase in thickness in order to cope with the demands made on the muscle. Different muscles in the body have different combinations of the number of slow and fast cells. People vary from one to another as regards the combination.

One player may be expected to have 80% slow and 20% fast cells in, for example, the knee extensor. Another might have 40% slow and 60% fast cells. These players will react quite differently to training programmes that contain, for example, condition training in the form of running and bodybuilding in the form of bounces.

MECHANICAL PROPERTIES OF THE MUSCLE

In detailed examinations it has been possible to show that a muscle can contract to about 50% of its initial length. A muscle has its greatest strength when it is extended to 20% longer than its normal resting length (d_0). The curve in **Figure 110** shows how much force a muscle can contract with, depending on the distance between its root and attachment.

You can easily test the accuracy of the curve by testing the strength of a friend; for example, at the positions 1, 2 and 3 shown in **Figure 110**. The person tries to pull in his lower leg while you are holding it to stop any movement. You could then say that you were measuring (feeling) his static strength in the three different positions.

Another mechanical property of a muscle is that it is stronger when it has to put the brake on a movement than when it has to initiate a movement. Thus it is claimed that a muscle is stronger when it works eccentrically (is pulled out) than when it works concentrically (contracts). Test this by getting a friend to sit behind you as in **Figure 111**. He should provide just enough resistance so that you can manage to pull in your lower leg towards your buttocks. See how strong you feel when you do this. Then compare with how strong you feel when you resist while your friend pulls (slowly) to stretch the knee. You will no doubt soon realise that you are stronger when resisting than when you are pulling your heels in yourself. We also know that the faster a movement is the harder it is to further increase its speed. For instance, if the lower leg moves at a certain speed, the force with which the muscles can increase that

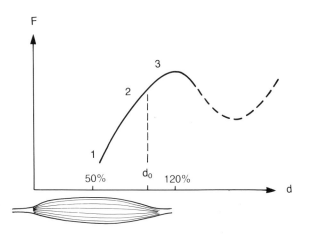

Figure 110

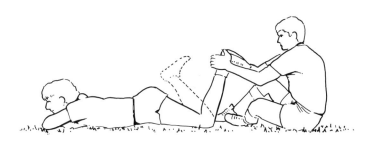

Figure 111

speed is very limited. This is comparable with a car engine, which has more reserves of power to increase speed from 30 to 40 mph than to increase it from 70 to 80 mph. A less natural and understandable observation is that a muscle is stronger in braking a movement than in starting it. This can be exploited so that when you want to get maximum force from a muscle, you first make a movement in the wrong direction. This 'counter-movement' has a braking effect, which gives impetus to great force (the elastic band effect) in the muscles which 'turn the movement round' and produces full starting power in the 'right direction'.

The curve which describes a muscle's maximum capacity at different speeds is drawn in **Figure 112**. The left-hand side of the curve shows the muscle's force when it is braking a movement (working eccentrically) and the right-hand side shows the force when the speed of movement is to be increased (working concentrically).

Test the above theory by jumping up (a) from a crouching position and (b) from a standing position with a starting movement down towards a crouching position immediately followed by jumping up, **Figure 113**. Experiment (a) corresponds to your starting the jump-up with a force which is less than the static maximum (see (a) in **Figure 113**).

Experiment (b) means that you can build up greater initial force; in other words, the jump-up begins with muscles that are already on 'maximum charge'.

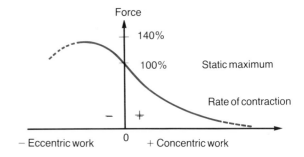

+ Means that the muscle becomes shorter.
0 Means that the muscle has not changed at all.
− Means that the muscle has become longer, though it tries to prevent this.

Figure 112

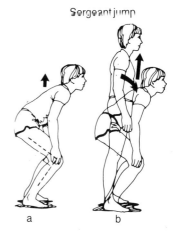

Sergeant jump

a   b

Figure 113 (a) Without a counter-movement. (b) With a counter-movement.

INCREASING MAXIMUM STRENGTH

If you can lift a maximum of 10 kilograms, as in **Figure 114**, 8 kilograms (that is 80% of the maximum weight) is usually about what it takes for you to get tired after 6 repeats (repetitions).

Rest a while and then take it through another 6 times, which constitutes one set. A normal training session to increase the strength of a muscle is usually 3 sets of 6 repetitions; that is, 18 repetitions with pauses in between. The pause should be 1–2 minutes long. You quickly learn how long you personally have to rest to be able to manage the next set of 6.

INCREASING STAYING POWER

Now try lifting a 4 kilogram weight: you will probably find that you can lift it about 40–50 times before you get tired. This type of training is called endurance training. After a few weeks you may be able to lift the same weight a 100 times before getting tired. If you then try to lift the 10 kilogram weight again, you will find that you have *not* become stronger: there has been no increase in your maximal dynamic strength. If we could look inside the muscle, we would see that the muscle cells are almost as thick as they were before but now they are surrounded by a finer network of capillaries, which gives the muscle more endurance.

The muscle cells you have trained are chiefly the oxygen-consuming slow cells. If you increase the loads and really tire out the muscle so that you 'can't manage' the last repeat, it is above all the fast fibres which are trained. These are made to work without access to oxygen, which means that energy and force are produced in a process which at the same time produces an inhibitory product for the muscle, called lactic acid. Too much lactic acid in the muscle produces pain and, finally, forces you to 'stop' and rest. Lactic acid is the body's way of preventing strain damage. In hard training, therefore, lactic acid is produced. The body, which has enzymes that break down the lactic acid into products that do not hinder the muscle's operation adjusts quite quickly to tolerating (breaking down) the lactic acid produced. You do not always need to have stages which produce lactic acid in the training: they can usefully be introduced a few weeks before the start of the series or when you expect to be able to produce top form over and above the usual.

Table 2 shows how to plan exercises to develop endurance (staying power), speed and maximal strength. The pauses between the sets should be so adjusted that you have the strength to execute the next set: 1–2 minutes is usually sufficient.

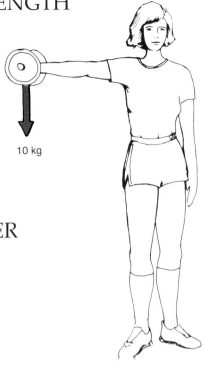

Figure 114

Table 2. Developing endurance, speed and strength.

	Endurance	Speed	Maximal strength
Per cent of maximum	25–50%	50–80%	80–100%
Repeats	> 40	~ 10	1–6
Number of sets	5	4	3

Training for any sport should always start with endurance training. With football, most of the training should aim at developing speed, which can be done with or without special equipment. Preferably, football training should be carried out within the team and without equipment. At the same time, you can then improve strength, balance and teamwork. And, above all, simultaneously working with many muscles improves coordination.

The most common exercises for strength training of the legs are now given. For each muscle that is important to footballers we give an exercise that is to be executed in the gym and also some exercises that give the same effect without equipment.

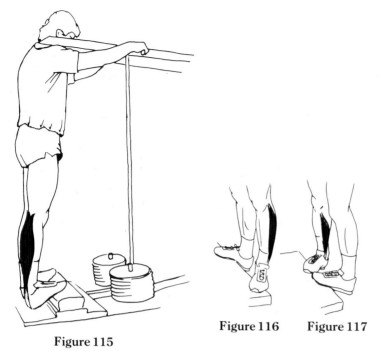

Figure 115

Figure 116   Figure 117

Figure 118

Figure 119

The calf muscle

To develop the calf muscle use different foot positions (**Figures 115–117**); this strengthens muscles that control the foot, which reduces the risk of spraining the ankle.

When you stand with your toes turned out (**Figure 116**) and rise up on the toes, the weight is on the big toe side of the foot. Thus, the foot is pronated and an extra load is placed on the muscles which, among other things, are designed to prevent twisting, which damages the ligament on the outside of the foot. If you stand with your toes turned in (**Figure 117**), and rise up on the toes so that your final position is with the weight out towards the little toes, the supinator is exercised.

If you practise exercises of the type shown in **Figures 118** to **121**, do not do more repetitions than you can do with maximal force. If you become tired and feel build-up you should rest, or train other muscles, before repeating the exercises. Elasticity exercises should be performed explosively—not slowly and exhaustedly. Do not jump too much on hard floors; use good shoes and, preferably, soft carpets to jump on if you are indoors. Lawns are naturally the best surface if you are training outdoors.

Skipping is a good way of training elasticity of the ankles and coordination. Vary the skipping as much as possible; for example, doing series of jumps on two legs, one leg, high jumps, jumps with high knee lifts, etc.

Figure 120

Figure 121

Too many jumping exercises on too hard a surface can easily lead to problems for the periosteum. Apart from strength and 'explosiveness', it is important to be well coordinated in your movements. In order to get an idea of what is meant by well coordinated, you should do the following exercise.

Standing on one leg, bend the free knee, keeping your arms folded so that you get no help from arm movements if you start losing your balance (**Figure 122**).

When you think that you are well balanced, close your eyes. If you are well coordinated, you should be able to stand still and only need to adjust your balance with small movements of your ankle. If you are poorly coordinated you will find it difficult to keep your balance. Try this exercise on both legs; if you have been injured recently (or seriously), you will probably find that your coordination (balance) on that leg is markedly less good. This, in turn, predisposes you to further injury of the same leg. After an injury, care should be taken in building up your strength, agility and coordination so the injured leg becomes as well trained as the healthy one.

Figure 122

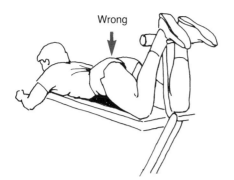

Figure 123

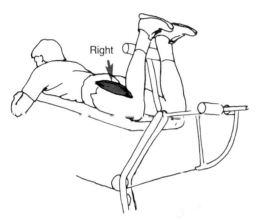

Figure 124

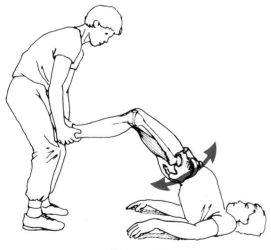

Figure 125

The knee flexors (back of the thigh)

The strength of the back of the thigh is very important to running speed. If you use the apparatus shown in **Figures 123** and **124**, make sure that you do not have weights heavier than you can manage without hollowing your back (lifting your buttocks).

It is better to train with low loads, using more repetitions, as this simulates the way the muscles are stressed during a game of football. Regular training prevents cramp and ruptures, and makes you faster at starts and short spurts. On the bodybuilding apparatus try pulling up the weight with both legs but brake the downward path with just one leg. You will soon realise that if the load is right for pulling up with two legs, then it is also right for resisting with one leg. As mentioned earlier, you are generally 40% stronger when you are braking than when you are getting up speed. Therefore, on any bodybuilding apparatus, you can expose the muscles to hard negative or eccentric training.

When the loads are too heavy you will notice that it is easier to manage the exercise if you hollow your back a little. However, this is not good because the muscle (iliopsoas) that allows you to do this has its root in the lumbar vertebrae. When the muscle is tensed hard it presses the vertebrae together at the same time and increases the pressure on the fragile discs. In the worst case hypothesis, you may be predisposing yourself to a slipped disc. The reason why you hollow your back when the loads are too heavy for the muscles on the back of the thigh is that by hollowing the back you lengthen the muscles at the back of the thigh. The root of that muscle group (the hamstrings) is the ischial tuberosity (tuber ischiadicum) and this is tipped away from the attachment down on the lower leg when you hollow your back. A muscle is stronger the further the distance is between the root and the attachment.

Figures 125–129 offer some suggestions as to how you can exercise the back of the thighs if you do not have access to apparatus. The exercises are chiefly of an endurance kind (apart from **Figure 127**), so you should do each exercise (whichever you choose) many times. For instance, do 3 times 20 repeats or 3 times 30, depending on when you get tired. You will need a helper to perform the following exercises.

Positioned as in **Figure 125**, drop your buttocks towards the floor and lift your hips up again by tensing the back of the thighs and the pelvic muscles. Pump up and down 20 to 30 times. Fall gently forwards with a straight body, as shown in **Figure 126**. Pull yourself back again with the help of the thigh muscles. This exercise is a strain. Make sure you are well warmed-up and do not lean too far forward to begin with: 10–20 drops per set might be about right.

Raise yourself up and drop down as in **Figure 125**, but this time use only one leg (**Figure 127**). The helper sits behind you (**Figure 128**), holding you round the heels and providing just sufficient resistance. Pull alternate legs towards you and resist when your partner pulls the leg back.

Run with quick back kicks towards your buttocks, trying to pull up your lower leg towards your buttocks as quickly as possible with each step (**Figure 129**).

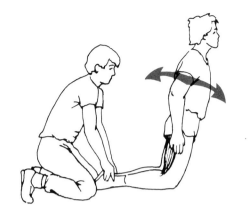

Figure 126

Figure 127

Figure 128

Figure 129

The knee extensors

In the exercise shown in **Figure 130** adjust the seat so that you start the exercise with an angle of 90° at the knee. This applies to all the exercises for the knee extensors. In **Figure 131**, adopt a position for the exercise similar to that used for the kick-off for starts and short spurts.

Some apparatus has a hydraulic arrangement that regulates the speed of the movement and can be adjusted to the required speed. You can read off on a meter how much force you are exerting. Decide how much force you want to exert and then make sure that you reach that level in every repetition.

In the exercises shown in **Figures 132** and **133** it is important not to bend the knees too much and not to work with a bent back.

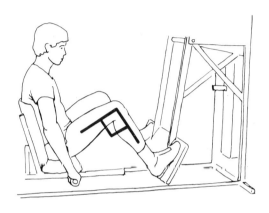

Figure 130

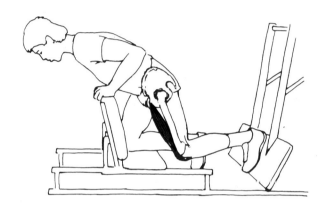

Figure 131

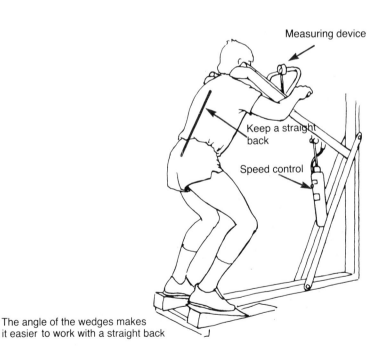

Measuring device

Keep a straight back

Speed control

The angle of the wedges makes it easier to work with a straight back

Figure 132

Keep a straight back

Figure 133

Do not put on more weights than you can straighten your knee completely with (**Figure 134**). Many people with 'weak knees' benefit from working regularly with this apparatus. They should only bend the knee 10–15° and then straighten the legs again. The knee must be exposed to relatively gentle stress, which means that you work between almost stretched and completely stretched positions.

In the exercises in **Figures 130, 132** and **133** you can brake on the return path with first one knee and then the other in order to achieve negative training. Stretching the knee is called positive (concentric) training, resisting on the way back is called negative (eccentric) training.

All the movements in the knee joint when you run, jump, brake, etc., are combined with movements in the hip joint. It is natural to stretch the knee and the hip simultaneously. When you kick a ball, however, you make a combination of movements that is 'unusual' for the body; namely, you stretch the knee and bend the hip. The training exercises described above are all of the natural knees stretch – hips stretch type, with the exception of the exercise shown in **Figure 134** in which the movement in the hip is disconnected. With apparatus you can build up the musculature so that you increase your power and run faster. If you want to kick harder, the best training method is still to practise kicking using many variations.

In the exercises shown in **Figures 130–133** the knee is subjected to the greatest stress when it is in the most bent position. This agrees with what happens when you jump up from a standing position, or in quick starts, etc. In the exercise shown in **Figure 134**, the stress is greatest with a stretched knee, which corresponds to the stress on the knee at the moment of impact in a kick. If you look more closely at the structure of the knee, you can see that three of the four quadriceps muscles pull the kneecap out slightly at an angle to the track in which the kneecap is to slide. The fourth muscle (the vastus medialis) pulls inwards at a very marked angle to counterbalance the three muscles pulling outwards (**Figure 135**). Imbalance in this system can easily give rise to instability in the knee and thus the consequent risk of knee injuries. The angle which is marked with a Q in **Figure 135** is wider for women (wider hips) than for men, which is why it is even more important for women to maintain the strength of the vastus medialis.

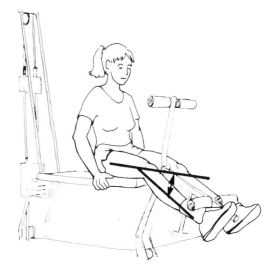

Figure 134

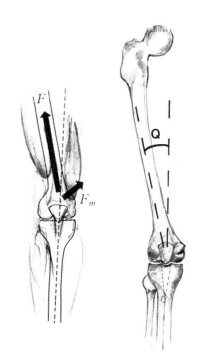

Figure 135

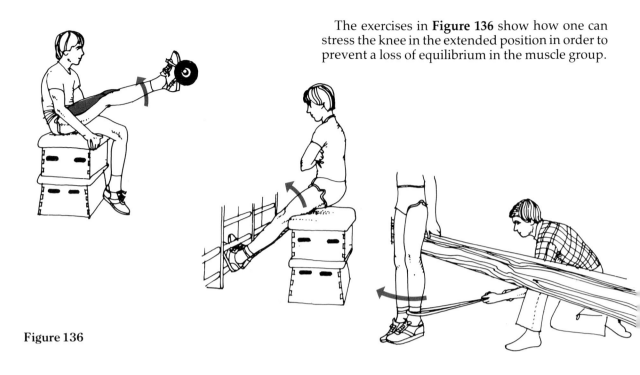

The exercises in **Figure 136** show how one can stress the knee in the extended position in order to prevent a loss of equilibrium in the muscle group.

Figure 136

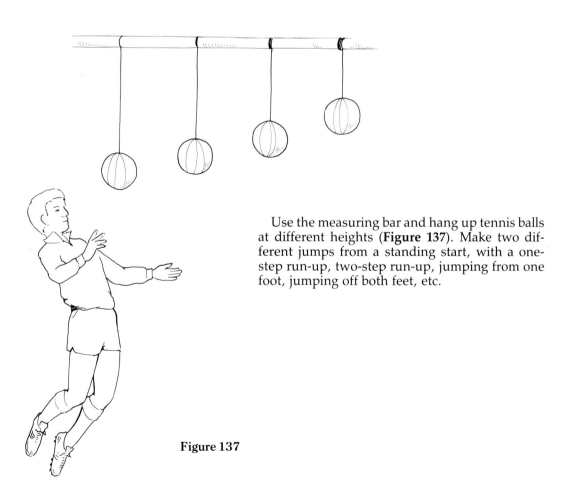

Use the measuring bar and hang up tennis balls at different heights (**Figure 137**). Make two different jumps from a standing start, with a one-step run-up, two-step run-up, jumping from one foot, jumping off both feet, etc.

Figure 137

EXERCISES FOR INCREASING POWER

Remember that all power training must be 'explosive'. Do not repeat too many times. Try to jump on a base such as turf, use good shoes and be aware of potential problems with the periosteum. Imagine you are standing in the middle of a big clock (**Figure 138**). Jump straight forwards (towards the number 12), land on your right foot and bounce quickly back to the middle again. Do that 3–4 times. Continue 3–4 times towards each imagined number. Turn your face towards the 12 the whole time. When you get to 6, change to the left leg.

Jump from side to side; for example, over a block. Do 4–5 explosive high jumps (**Figure 139**). Then rest a moment before repeating. Now jump 5–8 long jumps (**Figure 140**). Take a few steps, run and jump up as if for a header (**Figure 141**). Repeat many times.

When you are training the knee extensors and flexors you automatically train the hip flexors, groin muscles and pelvic muscles, especially when you do different sideways jumps.

Figure 138

Figure 139

Figure 140

Figure 142 shows the heights two different groups of jumpers reached after they had 'charged themselves up' by jumping down from different heights. For Group I, which consisted of people who had more than 60% slow muscle fibre in their knee flexor muscles, the greatest height, 41 cm, was reached after jumping down from 60 cm. For Group II, which consisted of people who had more than 60% fast muscle fibre in their knee flexor muscles, the best result was 37 cm from a jump down of 60 cm. The difference in suppleness was approximately 10%.

The curves show that if you jump down from a height of more than 60 cm, the result when jumping up again deteriorates. The best training height for the groups was setting the blocks at 60 cm (**Figure 143**).

If you jump down from too great a height you sink too far at the knee joints and end up in a position where you are weak (cf. **Figure 110**). If you jump down from too low a height you do not need to brake with your full force; that is, you do not 'charge up' the muscle to the full (cf. **Figure 112**).

We now consider examples of exercises that only stress the hip flexors (see **Figures 144–147**) and the groin muscles (see **Figures 148–151**).

Figure 141

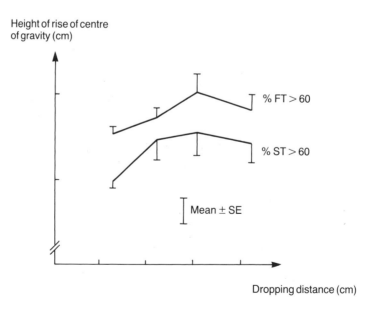

Figure 142

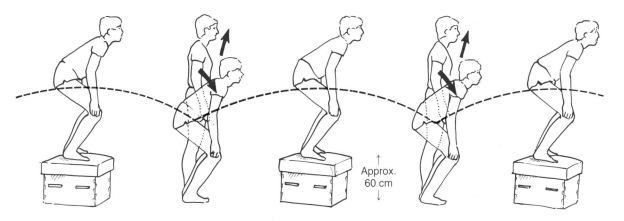

Figure 143

Approx.
60 cm

The hip flexors

Start with a stretched hip and the foot far back —
light load and 'soft start'. Then try to pull up your
knee as quickly and as high as you can (Figure
144)

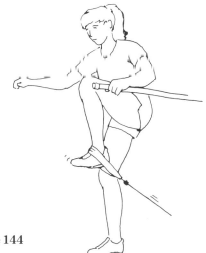

Figure 144

Quickly change legs and try to bring your knee
up to your chest each time (**Figure 145**).

Figure 145

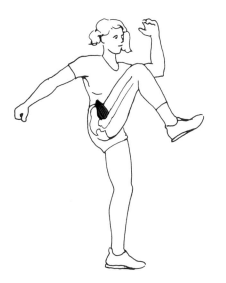

'War dance' with high knee raises (**Figure 146**). Jump off both feet with high knee raises (**Figure 147**).

The hip flexor musculature is entirely dominated by the iliopsoas (see **Figure 17**). This muscle is generally well trained and gets its training from fast running, start practice, running with changes of direction, acceleration training, etc. The problem is not usually that the player has hip flexors which are too weak but rather that the muscle group is too short and therefore creates problems in the lumbar region and the groin. So be careful with the stretching and agility training.

Figure 146

Figure 147

The groin muscles

In **Figure 148**, the string around the leg is attached to a weights machine. You should choose a weight so that you can do 10–15 repeats without getting too tired. Start with one foot out to the side and pull it towards and slightly across the foot you have your weight on. Held in the position shown in **Figure 149**, drop your hip down towards the floor and pull it up again. Pump up and down 10–15 times. Change sides.

Now we consider two static training exercises. Hold a ball between the knees as shown in **Figure 150**. Work with this type of exercise if you have had pains in the groin and want to train yourself up again. Do not try so hard that it hurts. **Figure 151** is a similar exercise to **Figure 150**, but involves another player rather than a ball. The player who has his knees on the outside is exercising his groin muscles, while the other player provides the appropriate resistance. Try to push each other slightly to and fro. Do not use maximum force but adjust to each other's strength.

In **Figure 148** you are training dynamically, pulling the weight towards you and then braking it on the way back. In **Figure 149** you are lifting up your hips from the floor and dropping back 10–15 times before you change sides; this is also dynamic training. In **Figures 150** and **151** you are training statically, pressing the knees inwards towards a resistance: in the first case, the ball is the resistance, while in the second your partner, who is constantly pushing outwards with his knees, is the resistance. Try the exercise in **Figure 151** and you will see in which direction you are strongest, pushing out or pushing in.

Strong and flexible groin muscles are especially important for footballers, which is why the above exercises, combined with stretching exercises, are needed in football training.

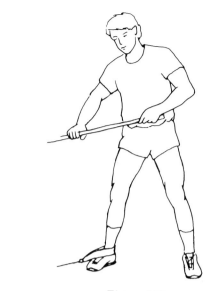

Figure 148

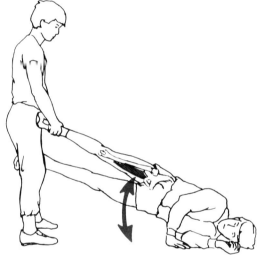

Figure 149

Figure 150

Figure 151

The hip extensors

Adopt the position shown in **Figure 152**, with one foot in front of the foot that is taking the weight; then push outwards. Lie on your side with legs together. Lift the top half of your body straight up sideways as high as you can (**Figure 153**), repeat 10–15 times. Change sides.

The pelvic muscles are exercised in all jumping, acceleration and running exercises. The gluteus maximus is active in any major exertions, while the gluteus medius and gluteus minimus are more responsible for coordination, balance and quick movements in the hip joint (see **Figures 4–6**). With a lot of running and jumping training the band of tendons, which stretches right from the crista iliaca (the iliac crest) and down to the outside of the tibia (shin bone), can become taut and foreshortened. This produces pain in the outer side of the knee because the bursa which lies between the thigh bone and the tendon is subjected to more friction than usual when the knee is bent and stretched. This phenomenon, which is called 'runner's knee', can be prevented with stretching exercises. **Figure 154** shows how the strong buttock muscle (gluteus maximus) and the tensor muscle of the fascia lata are attached to the iliotibial tract, a very strong tendon which glides along the outside of the thigh bone every time the knees bend.

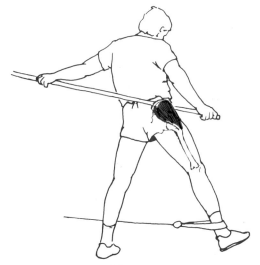

Figure 152

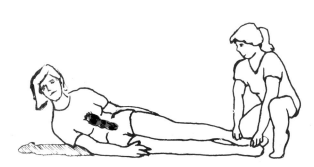

Figure 153

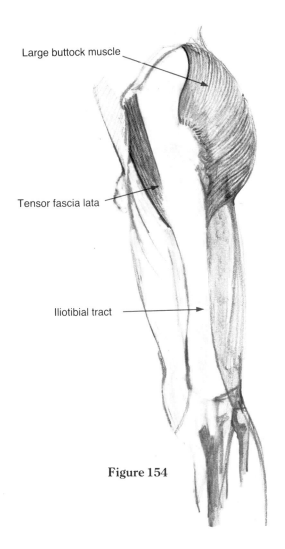

Large buttock muscle

Tensor fascia lata

Iliotibial tract

Figure 154

9 Training Back and Abdominal Muscles

As you by now appreciate, you cannot fully utilise the strength of your legs unless you also have strong back and abdominal muscles. Train regularly and choose exercises that make you stronger (able to do heavier and heavier exercises) and build up your stamina (increase your ability to do easier exercises more times). Abdominal muscle training is often more important than back muscle training; therefore, more suggestions for abdomen exercises are provided. The exercises are ordered in ascending degree of difficulty; that is, the easiest are shown first.

ABDOMEN EXERCISES

Positioned as in **Figure 155**, rise halfway up so that your right side is turned towards your left leg. Do not lie back prone on the ground but rise again and turn to the other side (your left side towards your right leg) before your head and shoulders reach the floor. Do 30–40 repeats.

Hold your legs still in the air. Roll slowly up and down. You are not supposed to jerk yourself up to a sitting position but slowly rise (by way of contracting your abdominal muscles) and come down slowly (**Figure 156**). Work against a wall, pressing your feet against it. Raise your upper body up and down, starting with the head (**Figure 157**). Position yourself as in **Figure 157**, but now with the legs straight (**Figure 158**). It is more difficult to 'roll up'.

Figure 155

Figure 156

Figure 157

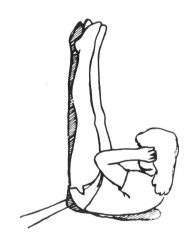

Figure 158

Figure 159

In the exercise shown in **Figure 159** the abdominal muscles are in action on the way up to I; from there, the hip flexors take over, up to II.

Abdominal muscle training can be done on a hard bench with the help of a partner (**Figure 160**) or you can lean the bench against a set of wall bars and put your feet between two bars. For another abdomen exercise, adopt the position shown in **Figure 161**, keeping the legs straight again. Press the small of your back against the floor as you go up and down.

Figure 162 is a variant of the exercise shown in **Figure 160**; both exercises are hard work. You can

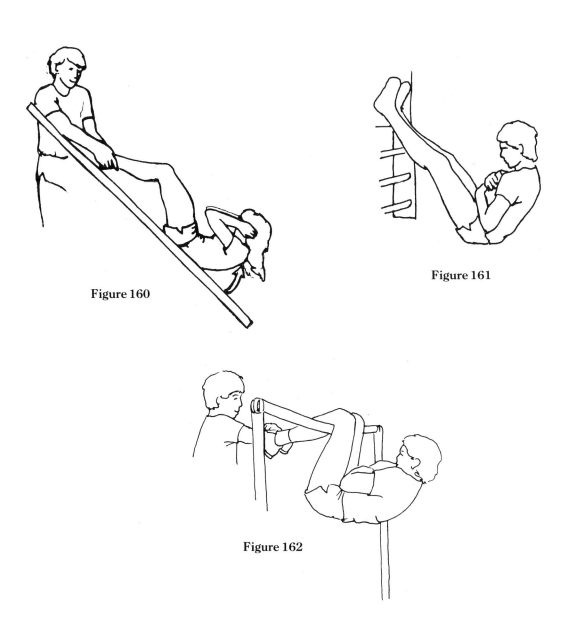

Figure 160

Figure 161

Figure 162

exercise the oblique stomach muscles by turning around with the help of a strong elastic support, as shown in **Figure 163**. Now adopt the position shown in **Figure 164** by dropping forward on to your hands, placing them far away from your feet and walking on the spot with both hands and feet; this will provide very tough exercise for the stomach. Now, drop forward on to your hands and hop so that you are supported on the right and left legs alternately (**Figure 165**). The forward leg must not touch the ground. This exercise is very hard work!

There are three more abdomen exercises to describe in this section. Lie on your back with your arms pressed against the floor. Lift your knees straight up towards the ceiling so that your buttocks lift a few centimetres off the floor (**Figure 166**). Work gently without jerking. Can you manage it? It is difficult to get as high as in **Figure 166**.

Hang from a crossbar and roll up so that your knees come up to your forehead (**Figure 167**). Roll up gently. No jerky movements! Repeat the exercise in **Figure 167**, but now keep the legs straight (**Figure 168**); this makes it more difficult. The exercises in **Figures 167** and **168** are demanding for both the stomach muscles and the hip flexors.

Figure 163

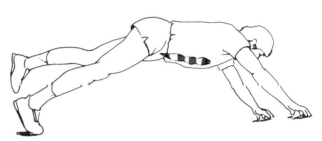

Figure 164

Figure 165

Figure 166

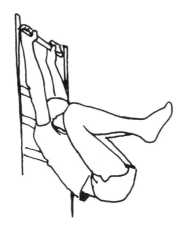

Figure 167

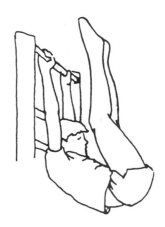

Figure 168

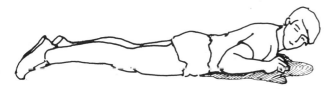

Figure 169

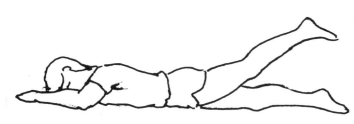

Figure 170

BACK MUSCLE EXERCISES

All exercises which train the back muscles must be done *slowly without jerking!*

- Lie on your stomach. Slowly lift the top half of your body as high as you can (**Figure 169**). Stay there for 6–8 seconds while turning slightly, look at your heels and rotate. Then drop back to the floor again. Repeat 5–6 times.
- Lift one leg at a time and take it back again, slowly, rhythmically and without jerking (**Figure 170**). Repeat 10–20 times each leg.
- Get down on all fours. Lift one arm and the opposite leg as high as you can (**Figure 171**). Hold it for 6–8 seconds; then do 8–10 repeats, changing sides.
- Stand with a straight back but dropping forward. Do swimming movements with your arms (**Figure 172**). Exercise for 30–40 seconds.

Figure 171

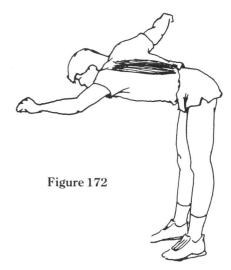

Figure 172

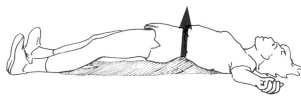

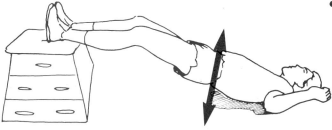

- Lie prone on your back, or with feet on a box (**Figure 173**). Push your hips up as far as you can. Drop back. Exercise 10–20 times.
- Adopt position shown in **Figure 174** and hop with left and right legs alternately. Keep your hips up as high as you can.
- Jump from a standing position with one arm around a partner's shoulders, into his arms and down again (**Figure 175**). Repeat 10–15 times.
- With a little imagination players can train together and make up exercises that are a bit more fun (**Figure 176**).

Figure 173

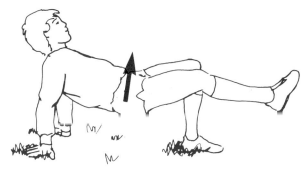

Figure 174

Figure 175

Figure 176

10 General Strength Training

Having gone through the various strength and flexibility exercises given in earlier chapters, you are probably better positioned to understand exercises that are directly related to football. Our aim is that you should become more flexible and quicker and, thus, a better player.

We now give you examples of general strength training programmes composed of exercises detailed earlier. The exercises chosen do not require strength training equipment; they are meant to be practised indoors during the off-season and programmes should take 20 minutes. Be careful to warm-up properly before you start training.

TRAINING PROGRAMMES

We now give 10 suggested programmes that involve working alternately with the legs, abdomen and back. At each stage you have 2 different exercises to choose from. You work for 30 seconds, rest for 30 seconds and work again for 30 seconds, followed by a second pause for 30 seconds. During the second pause you prepare yourself for the next stage. A good idea could be to record music on tape where the music is loud for 30 seconds while you are working and low for 30 seconds while you are resting. Thus, 20–30 people could train at the same time. Everyone will then know when to work, rest and change.

The 10 suggested programmes:

1. Legs (**Figures 177** and **178**).
2. Abdomen (**Figures 179** and **180**).
3. Back (**Figures 181** and **182**).
4. Legs (**Figures 183** and **184**).
5. Abdomen (**Figures 185** and **186**).
6. Arms (**Figures 187** and **188**).
7. Legs (**Figures 189** and **190**).
8. Abdomen (**Figures 191** and **192**).
9. Back (**Figures 193** and **194**).
10. Legs (**Figures 195** and **196**).

1 Legs

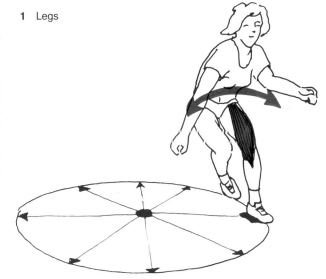

Figure 177

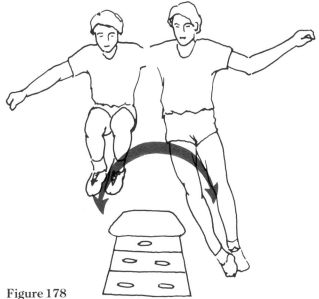

Figure 178

2 Abdomen

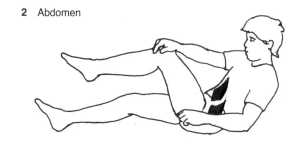

Figure 179

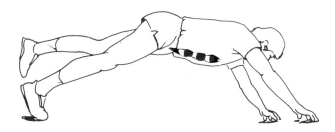

Figure 180

3 Back

Figure 181

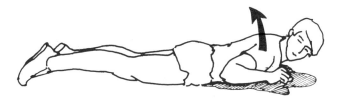

Figure 182

4 Legs

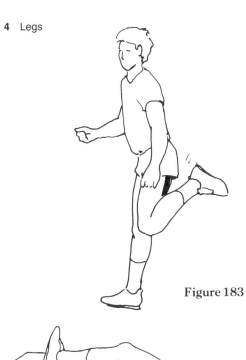

Figure 183

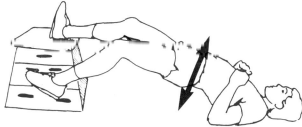

Figure 184

5 Abdomen

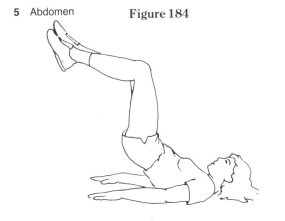

Figure 185

Figure 186

Figure 187

Figure 188

7 Legs

Figure 189

Figure 190

8 Abdomen

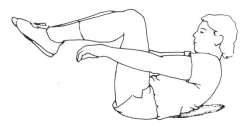

Figure 191

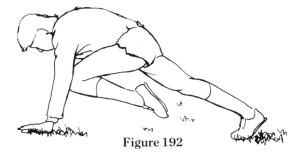

Figure 192

9 Back

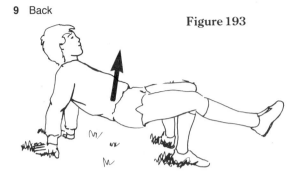

Figure 193

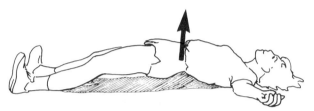

Figure 194

10 Logo

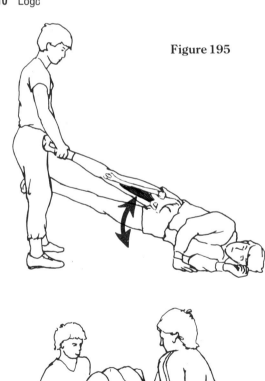

Figure 195

Figure 196

DESIGN YOUR OWN EXERCISES

The exercises which have been suggested can be easily replaced with similar ones as you tire of them. The idea is that they should provide an all-round form of bodybuilding training. It should also be possible to use them for warming-up and limbering-up before a training session. One circuit with 30-second pauses lasts 20 minutes. Two circuits represent a good solid training session. If you only take one of the variations suggested without pauses in between, it is a good warm-up lasting 5 minutes. Try it out and see how you can best apply the suggestions for your team. If you have the use of indoor accommodation for winter training it would perhaps be appropriate for half the team to play while the other half does general bodybuilding exercises. In this way you can increase efficiency both in the game and in the time when you cannot play for reasons of space.

If you want to practise pure bodybuilding, such as using disc bars, dumbbells, etc., to give yourself good basic strength, in parallel with that training you should also do some agility training and some power training to make sure that your strength is adapted to football.

EXAMPLES OF SYSTEMATIC STRENGTH TRAINING

Some girls from a team in the first division did leg-strengthening and stamina-enhancing exercises for a period of 15 weeks during the off-season. They hoped that this would improve their ability to last the match while giving them a better chance of avoiding injury. Their training sessions included several different leg exercises but here we analyse the results of only one of these exercises.

Leg muscle training

First, maximal strength was tested using the apparatus shown in **Figure 197**. On average, the girls managed to press 90 kilograms, so their maximum was set to 90 kg. Next, they were tested on how many times they could manage with a workload of 45 kg i.e. 50%, before getting tired. The result was 50 times on average.

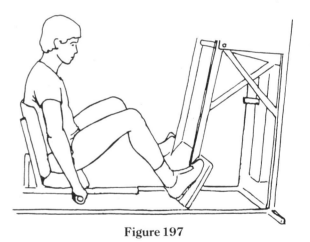

Figure 197

Endurance and maximal strength training

During the first 15 training sessions (3 times a week for 5 weeks) they trained at 50% of capacity, i.e. using a workload of 45 kg. They did 3 sets of exercises, each consisting of 15 repetitions, i.e. 3 × 15 for the first 5 sessions, then 4 × 15 for the next 5 sessions, and finally 5 × 15 for the last 5 sessions. Consequently, they started training with relatively light workloads and a relatively small number of repetitions. The number of repetitions was then increased as the time went by. During this period we expected them to accustom their joints, ligaments and muscles to the exercises. We expected a possible increase of endurance but no increase of maximal strength.

As regards maximal strength, the result of the re-test after 5 weeks was the same as on the first test (before training), i.e. 90 kilograms. When the girls' endurance was tested, however, they could do 85 repetitions before getting tired, which is a much better endurance.

The following 5-week period they trained with heavier workloads. The training sessions were as follows:

3 × 6 (70% of 90 kg) for 5 sessions
3 × 6 (80% of 90 kg) for 5 sessions
4 × 6 (80% of 90 kg) for 5 sessions

After the 5-week period the girls could press a maximum weight of 120 kg and do 120 repetitions with a workload of 45 kg.

The last 5 weeks they trained with 50% of their maximum, but this time of their new maximum, which was 120 kg. Fifty per cent of 120 kg means a workload of 60 kg. Their task was now to do a certain number of repetitions which we thought was suitable partly for endurance training and partly for maximal strength training. We assumed that they would be so tired at the end of each set that the last few repetitions would be pure strength training.

This programme comprised:

3 × 30 (60 kg) for 5 sessions
4 × 40 (60 kg) for 5 sessions
5 × 50 (60 kg) for 5 sessions

The results of the final test showed that they had acquired a maximal strength of 150 kg and the endurance to press 45 kg 190 times. Forty-five kilograms was kept as a workload in the different endurance tests throughout the 15 weeks in order to be able to compare the test results with the original test.

Thus, over the 15-week period (45 sessions) there was an increase of maximal strength from 90 to 150 kg and an increase of endurance from 50 to 190 repetitions with a workload of 45 kg (**Table 3**).

Table 3. Summary of results.

	Before training	After 15 sessions	After 30 sessions	After 45 sessions
Maximum strength (kg)	90	90	120	150
Endurance with a workload of 45 kg (repetitions)	50	85	120	190

We feel that our results show that these girls were better prepared to withstand strains and stresses, particularly on those muscles that had been subjected to this training, and thereby more resistant to injury. A well-thought out programme that includes the most important muscles, together with flexibility and elasticity exercises, should be a way of keeping fit during the off-season and of developing a well-trained body for 16–18 year olds who wish to follow a career in football.

TRAINING MODEL FOR LEG MUSCLES

The exercises outlined below constitute a suggestion for well-balanced training for the legs. To these you should add stomach, back and arm exercises of a more general nature. It is appropriate to take one leg exercise, one stomach exercise, one leg exercise, one back exercise, one leg exercise, etc.

For the leg exercises you can follow the training model below. First measure your maximum strength and your endurance (50% of your maximum strength). Then start with the first 5 training sessions doing 15 repetitions in 3 sets with 50% of your maximum weight. Increase by one set every fifth session:

5 sessions 3 × 15 (50%)
5 sessions 4 × 15 (50%)
5 sessions 5 × 15 (50%)

Now here are some examples of exercises (**Figures 198–203**):

After these 15 sessions measure your maximum strength and your staying power again. For the next 15 weeks take 70–80% of your latest maximum.

5 sessions 3 × 6 (70%)
5 sessions 3 × 6 (80%)
5 sessions 4 × 6 (80%)

Measure again

5 sessions 3 × 30 (50%)
5 sessions 4 × 40 (50%)
5 sessions 5 × 50 (50%)

Measure again. Fill out a new table for each exercise so that the training results can be easily seen.

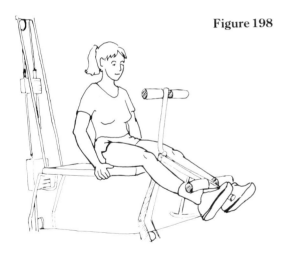

Figure 198

	Before training	After 15 sessions	After 30 sessions	After 45 sessions
Maximum strength				
Endurance (with 50% of *first* max. strength)				
Endurance (with 50% of *new* max. strength)				

Figure 199

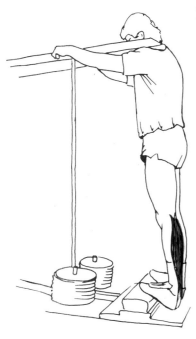

	Before training	*After 15 sessions*	*After 30 sessions*	*After 45 sessions*
Maximum strength				
Endurance (with 50% of *first* max. strength)				
Endurance (with 50% of *new* max. strength)				

Figure 200

	Before training	*After 15 sessions*	*After 30 sessions*	*After 45 sessions*
Maximum strength				
Endurance (with 50% of *first* max. strength)				
Endurance (with 50% of *new* max. strength)				

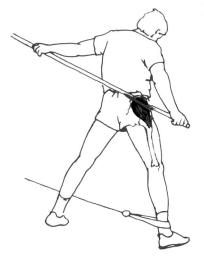

Figure 201

	Before training	*After 15 sessions*	*After 30 sessions*	*After 45 sessions*
Maximum strength				
Endurance (with 50 % of first max. strength)				
Endurance (with 50% of *new* max. strength)				

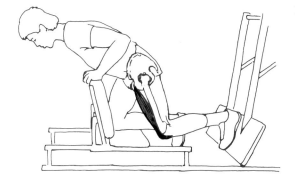

Figure 202

	Before training	*After 15 sessions*	*After 30 sessions*	*After 45 sessions*
Maximum strength				
Endurance (with 50% of *first* max. strength)				
Endurance (with 50% of *new* max. strength)				

Figure 203

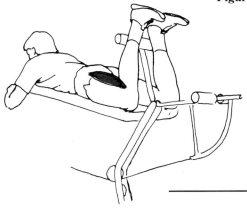

	Before training	After 15 sessions	After 30 sessions	After 45 sessions
Maximum strength				
Endurance (with 50% of *first* max. strength)				
Endurance (with 50% of *new* max. strength)				

In each session you should remember to:

- Warm-up properly before you begin.
- Pay attention to any pains which suggest strain.
- Mix the leg exercises with a stomach exercise, a back exercise and some arm exercises; for example, those suggested in **Figures 204–207**.

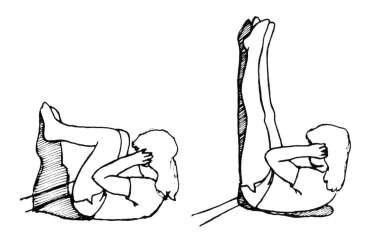

Figure 204

Figure 205

Figure 206

Figure 207

● Finish each session with relatively precise stretching exercises, for example, in the 6 positions shown in **Figures 208–213**. It is better to stretch, i.e. pull a relaxed muscle for 30 seconds, than to use the contraction–relaxation–stretching method. This applies after all hard training.

Figure 208

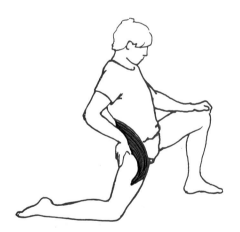

Figure 209

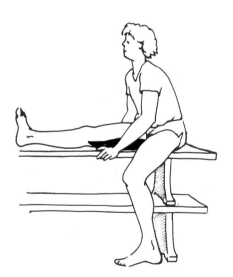

Figure 210

Figure 211

Figure 212

Figure 213

CONTINUING STRENGTH TRAINING DURING THE FOOTBALL SEASON

If you practise the exercises we have outlined or similar exercises out of season, then during the football season you should continue the strength training, but perhaps just once a week and with other exercises. The exercises should be of the speed and power type, and should be done on the football pitch. So try to keep your new found strength by forcing your body to maximum exertion in at least one session per week for each muscle group. Maximum means in terms of strength — not staying power. The exercises may be of the type described in the general strength training programme on pages 65–75.

Do not worry if some of the strength you have gained from the off-season training disappears during the football season. This is natural. Not all of your newly won strength is directly suited to the type of activity which football involves, and that is why you will lose it. The strength you retain is the type which your football playing maintains; that is, strength adapted to football — the strength that makes you run faster, jump higher and kick harder. The curve shown in **Figure 214** is a theoretical model for the way your strength may vary during the season. The more power and speed-oriented playing exercises you do during the playing season, the more of your newly won strength will stay with you.

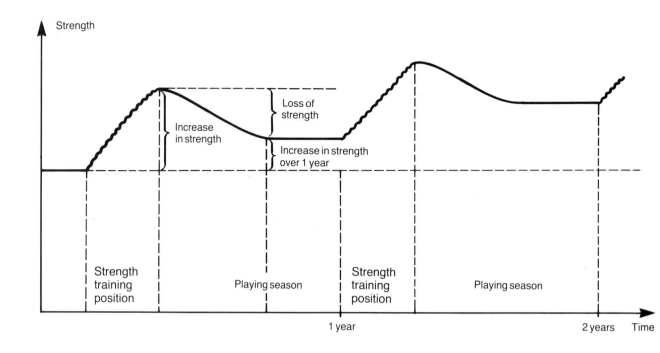

Figure 214

CONCLUDING REMARKS

This method of first analysing which muscles are being used in a certain sport, and then finding out whether it is strength in certain muscles which is needed and agility in others, can undoubtedly be applied to most sports. Today, each athlete aiming for the top trains so much that it is important that their time be well spent. This means that you must be precise about what muscles you train and how you train them.

If you are interested in how the body works in the athletic context you can obtain more information by reading the book *Athletic Ability and the Anatomy of Motion*, also published by Wolfe. This will give you more ideas.

Good luck with your training!

Rolf Wirhed

Glossary

The following words may have different interpretations in different fields. Their meanings in *this book* are defined.

Agility training
Agility training consists of different methods of maintaining or increasing the body's agility. Extensions, swaying movements in extreme positions, stretching and contraction methods are all included in agility training.

Concentric strength
If the muscle contracts and tries to increase the speed of the part of the body it is attached to, we say that the muscle is working concentrically.

Contraction method
This term actually stands for agility training in the form of the contraction–relaxation–stretching method. You contract the muscle for 6 seconds in an extreme position — relax, still in the extreme position, for 2 seconds — and then extend (stretch) for 10 seconds.

Dynamic strength
Dynamic strength means that the muscle is working and either contracting, i.e. increasing the speed of the part of the body it is attached to, or expanding and therefore trying to brake the part of the body it is attached to.

Eccentric strength
If a muscle is pulled away by a part of the body which is moving, but the muscle is trying to prevent this — i.e. the muscle is trying to put the brake on that part of the body — we say that the muscle is working eccentrically. A muscle is always stronger when it can work eccentrically than when it is working concentrically.

Explosive strength
Explosive strength enables you to start quickly, reach maximum speed quickly, brake quickly, jump high, etc.

Lactic acid
Lactic acid is a compound formed in a muscle that has to produce energy in the absence of oxygen, i.e. overworking. If the level of lactic acid is too high, pain is experienced and use of the muscle should cease.

Power
A powerful player jumps high, quickly reaches maximum speed and is good at braking, turning and changing direction.

Static strength
Static (or isometric) strength is a term which describes how a muscle tenses and tries to move. However, because other, equally strong, forces are resisting it, no movement occurs in the joint

Stretching
Stretching means extending, and is used to describe the agility training which involves remaining still for about 30 seconds with a relaxed, extended muscle. The force with which you extend the muscle must not be too great, so it should not hurt! It is very important to really stretch for 30 seconds and not stop after 10–15 seconds.

Supple
A supple player is both strong and agile.

Index